This book is for you, the reader. May it inspire you to break free from whatever holds you back so you may begin living life unbound.

Published by: Life Unbound Publishing,
http://unboundva.com

Cover design: Valentina Mucci, Parentesi Graphics
http://parentesigraphica.it

Interior design: John DuBois, Life Unbound Publishing
http://lifeunboundpublishing.com

Printed by: CreateSpace, An Amazon.com Company

1st edition, November 2013

ISBN-13: 978-0615924342
ISBN-10: 0615924344

Printed in the United States of America

Living Life Unbound: The Passions That Drive Female Entrepreneurs

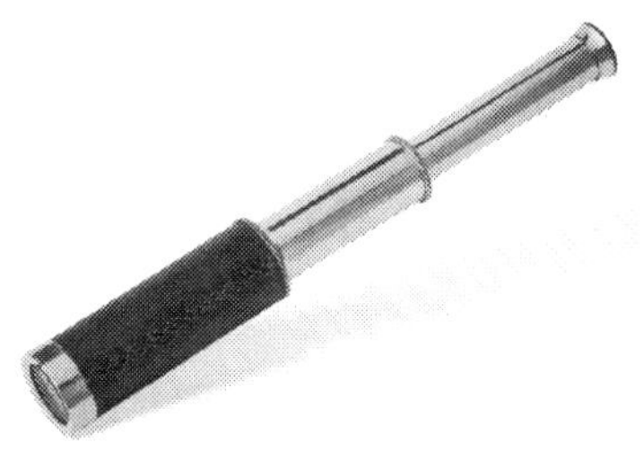

Edited by:

Tara DuBois
Tara Ursulescu
John DuBois

Life Unbound Publishing
Oregon, USA

Table of Contents

FOREWORD **9**

INTRODUCTION **11**

PART 1: HELPING OTHERS **15**

FROM HEADSHOTS TO HEALER: MY PATH TO BECOMING A SHAMAN
BY MIKKI BALOY 19

THE SONG OF THE SAW
BY PATT GREGORY 27

IT'S OKAY AND YOU ARE NOT ALONE: SHARING THE CHALLENGES OF ENTREPRENEURSHIP
BY SU-MARI DU BRUYN 35

COMPELLED TO FOLLOW MY DREAMS
BY LENA KENNEDY 41

LIVE WITH INTENTION
BY JUANITA ARRANT 47

QUITTING THE CORPORATE MONKEY JUNGLE
BY LISA LANDTROOP 53

PART 2: EXPERIENCING A WAKE-UP CALL **57**

THE PASSION HIDDEN WITHIN ME
BY CHRIS BLEVINS 61

MI HISTORIA
BY GRETEL LINDBLOOM 69

FILLING MY GYPSY SPIRIT
BY HALEY HINES. 77

BEYOND THE 9 TO 5: HOW I BECAME A MOONLIGHTING ENTREPRENEUR
BY JEANNIE SPIRO 85

SEEING MY LIFE WITH MY OWN EYES
BY SARA JAMES WILLIAMS 91

CHANGING MY FOCUS
BY SHARI YANTES 99

PART 3: DRIVE TO FULFILL PURPOSE 105

THE LINE IN THE SAND
BY KERRY SWETMON 109

IN MEMORIAM: ADA AUSTIN 121

LET GO AND LIVE, BECAUSE...NOW I AM BIG!
BY CONNIE LARSON 127

LETTING GO AND EMBRACING THE "NOW"
BY MARY SOMMERSET 135

FLEXING MY COURAGE MUSCLE
BY CAROL LEBLANC 143

IT'S ALL ABOUT PASSION!
BY TARA URSULESCU 149

PART 4: LIFE BY YOUR OWN DESIGN 159

ON LETTING YOURSELF BE SEEN
BY MADELEINE ENO 163

A LIFE OF ART, MUSIC, AND SMILES
BY LESLIE ANN AKIN 171

COACHING OF THE MIND: MY PATH AS A HYPNOTIST
BY LISA SMITH......179

MAKING IT POSSIBLE MY OWN WAY
BY MARY JOYCE......187

BE CAREFUL WHAT YOU WISH FOR
BY RACHELLE FREEGARD......195

A LIFE UNBOUND FROM REGRET
BY TARA DUBOIS......201

AFTERWORD 207

ABOUT THE EDITORS 209

Foreword

"Somewhere between the shadows of yesterday and the shade of tomorrow is a place where dreams are born and souls awaken." - Veronica Drake

Instantly I found myself drawn to the courageousness that fills every page in this beautifully inspiring book. I also willingly and fondly journeyed back through all of my own transformations - with a smile on my face and warmth in my heart.

This book represents the collective voice of women everywhere who know there is more than what they are living day-to-day.

Stories of freedom, hope, transformation and soulful connections are woven throughout. You quickly realize dreams are not attached to a by-when date. Society gives us those benchmarks but our souls aren't willing to conform. Our expiration date is not an earthly determination and until there is no more breath in our physical body we are on a mission to unite with our soul and birth our true purpose. This book gives us the inspiration to do just that.

Death..Disease..Disaster.. Divorce - The four D's. One of these D's will come into each of our lives and will rock our world like never before. Each of the women in this book has had an intimate experience with a "D" and she has risen above the challenge and accepted the role of teacher. Sharing her story so that it might offer some hope to someone who is dreaming, suffering or ready to change.

If you are struggling with finding the courage to live life on your terms I highly recommend this book. Everyone's journey is different and every individual must listen for their own beat. It sure is comforting to know the road has been traveled by so many amazing women.

Veronica Drake
Intuitive Business Consultant
http://veronicadrake.com

Introduction

Do you have a passion burning deep inside you calling you to follow it? Do you have a dream of leaving your conventional career behind and striking out on your own? If so, you are not alone.

The dynamics of the business world are changing. Fed up by the economy, inflexible corporate structures, or just a plain desire to create and be heard, many individuals have eschewed the traditional career path to start their own business and live a life of their own design.

Women in particular have played a huge role in this new look of business. Frustrated by glass ceilings and working in male dominated organizations, professional women continue to leave traditional work structures in droves to stake out on their own.

This phenomenon has taken place worldwide. Between 1997 and 2013 the number of women-owned enterprises grew at 1 ½ times the national average in the United States.[1] In the United Kingdom women entrepreneurs

---

[1] American Express OPEN. (2013) *2013 State of Women-Owned Business Report: A summary of Trends, 1997-2013*. Retrieved from: https://c401345.ssl.cf1.rackcdn.com/wp-content/uploads/2013/03/13ADV-WBI-E-StateOfWomenReport_FINAL.pdf

have contributed to over half of the increase in small business ownership since 2008.[2] Since 2000, there has been a 21.7% increase in the number of Australian women who run their own businesses.[3]

Knowing well the passion that burns inside us, we wondered what drove all of these other women entrepreneurs to leave the conventional workforce and stake out on their own. Sure, we had broad, general reasons provided by surveys and research, but we wanted to hear the personal stories behind these courageous decisions. What motivated these women to take action? What sparked the passion that powers their entrepreneurial drive?

We asked female small business owners from around the world to share the catalyst that compelled them to leave their old lives behind so they could pursue their passions and live authentically. We call this "living life unbound."

For us, "living life unbound" means having the freedom to design the life-work balance of one's own choosing. It means breaking free from traditional thought processes, conventional business practices, society expectations, and whatever else holds you back and prevents you from progressing. It means finding true happiness and balance in both your personal and professional lives by

---

2 Office of National Statistics. (2013) *Labour Force Survey*. (ONG Persistent Identifier 10.5255/UKDA-SN-7277-1).

3 Sammartino, Andre. (2013). Australia's Underestimated Resource: Women Doing Business Globally. *Women in Global Business*. Retrieved from: http://www.academia.edu/4084677/Australias_Underestimated_Resource_Women_Doing_Business_Globally

following that voice inside of you guiding you to soul satisfaction. It means turning your dreams into reality. After putting out the call for stories online, we received personal testimonials from women around the world. We were amazed and inspired by each woman's unique path to living a life unbound and of her own choosing. From these outstanding responses we created this book.

We broke down this book into four parts, with each one representing a specific theme. We noticed that while each story was unique, when it came to what sparked the passion that powers their entrepreneurial drive, women mentioned a desire to help others, experiencing a wake up call, being driven to fulfill a purpose, or a yearning to live a life of their own design. We organized the book based around those natural groupings.

Proceeds from the sale of this book will go to the non-profit organization Kiva Microfunds, based out of San Francisco, California. Kiva operates an online lending platform that facilitates loans for low-income entrepreneurs and students in 70 countries. With over 80% of Kiva's loans helping women from across the globe start their own small businesses, we felt that the mission of this organization matched well with our values and overarching theme of helping women live their lives unbound. To learn more about Kiva and to read personal stories of those helped by this microfinancing institution, please visit www.kiva.org.

Please enjoy this book as much as we did putting it together. Whether you seek motivation to start your own endeavor or just enjoy reading positive tales of feminine strength, these stories will both warm your heart and embolden your spirit.

Get inspired so you can break free from what holds you back and live your life unbound!

Part 1: Helping Others

The world can be a very competitive place. It can often feel as if people just look out for their own interests and give little thought to others. We, as individuals, get so wrapped up in our own lives and our attempts to get ahead that we lose touch with the people around us.

Yet, when we slow down and take a hard look we find the opposite is true: little bits of humanity and altruism are being practiced everywhere. Whether it's coordinated drives for charity, random acts of generosity, or simply neighbors looking out for neighbors, kindness is all around us.

When conducting research for this book we noticed a recurring theme from those who responded. These women were driven by an inherent need to help others. They feel as if they are called on to do more in this world than to just work a traditional job pushing paper. These people want to make a positive impact on the lives of others.

We heard about that drive in the stories we collected. One author shares her very personal journey from being near ground zero during the September 11th, 2001 attacks in New York City to becoming a spiritual shaman.

Another relates how she broke into male-dominated field and now dedicates her life to helping other women do the same.

Many entrepreneurs desire to pay forward a type of mentor relationship that benefited them. Others provide advice to newcomers that they would have liked to have heard when they were first starting out. Our selections share stories that match those motivations as well.

We certainly understand those sentiments. A big part of this book is helping others live life unbound. We derive a deep satisfaction from helping others break free from what holds them back. By helping others create better lives for themselves we in turn create a better society in which we all can live.

As you read through these stories ask yourself how you can make a positive difference in your community and to the others around you. What legacy will you leave behind? How will you pay forward the kindness that has been shown to you?

Even making a small change can have an impact. If we all do little things big things can happen. Smile at your neighbors and lend a helping hand. Break free of the "me-first" mindset and live a life unbound.

"I had a pretty major case of post-traumatic stress disorder, complete with panic attacks, nightmares, and a depression that sucked all the laughter out of me. Acting didn't matter anymore, because nothing did."

- Mikki Baloy

From Headshots to Healer: My Path to Becoming a Shaman

By Mikki Baloy

People often ask how a "white girl" from the Catskills became a shamanic healer. This certainly wasn't my major in college. Truth is, I used to be an actress, doing the starving-artist thing like a champ in New York City. Somehow my shy, little 23-year-old self subsisted on bagels that were four-for-a-dollar at the corner bodega while I worked day jobs I hated, auditioned a lot, and did plays that no one saw. In other words, I was living the dream.

Then, just shy of my first anniversary in the city, the September 11th attacks on the World Trade Center happened. I was downtown. *There.* I'll spare you the darker details but that afternoon, I walked the Brooklyn Bridge back to my friend's place, where I was crashing on a futon and living out of a suitcase. When I went back to my receptionist job on Wall Street a few days later, guys in hazmat suits were cleaning inch-thick dust off of window ledges while I strolled by in pantyhose and discount-store flats.

Suffice it to say, I had a pretty major case of post-traumatic stress disorder, complete with panic attacks, nightmares, and a depression that sucked all the laughter out of me. Acting didn't matter anymore, because *nothing* did. I didn't plan more than three days in advance because I didn't feel safe enough to look forward to anything. Friends invited me to get out of town and I kept putting them off. I couldn't explain to them why I felt like planning for pleasure was simply a way to tempt fate. When I got laid off from the Wall Street gig in 2003, a friend hooked me up with an administrative job at a 9/11 foundation. Eager for anything resembling a paycheck, I took the job, not realizing how important it would become in the larger arc of my life.

I worked there for eight years, creating and maintaining programs that helped thousands of people with long-term recovery. Our work included emergency financial assistance, social work and mental health programs, education to help pastors recognize the post-disaster rise in domestic violence, day-camps for kids who were affected (and starting to ask hard questions), and a lot more. I was part of healing the city.

Quite a day job for an actress.

Through the foundation, I also had access to some of the best trauma therapists in the country, and very quickly recovered fully from the PTSD and depression. I had the honor of being part of the resiliency of my adopted home, and simultaneously learned first-hand about my *own* capacity to heal.

When the agency closed in 2008, acting just didn't feel like the right thing anymore. I grieved the loss of that dream and wondered what would come next. It was such a puzzling time that I went to Kripalu, a retreat center in the Berkshires, in an effort to clear my head.

As Fate would have it, the days I had booked to just get away and rest were the exact days that a shaman was teaching an introductory workshop.

Shamanism is ancient energy medicine, a whole system of creating balance and restoring wholeness in mind, body, and spirit. I'd been mildly interested in it for most of my life, having always felt a deep and abiding connection to the woods near my house, and to all of Nature. When I was a child, I got really sick with what may have been undiagnosed Lyme Disease, and spent the better part of a summer steeping in fever dreams that I was told were "only hallucinations." In retrospect, they were actually visions, contact with the ordinarily unseen world of energy and spirit.

Throughout my young adulthood, I read Joseph Campbell and studied religion, searching for language for what I felt and knew to be true of my place in the world. In all my searching, I discovered a resonance with both Eastern Philosophy and shamanism. I studied Buddhism for several years and kept shamanic journeying and ideas of contact with the spirit world in my back pocket.

So, later, I signed up for that Kripalu class on a whim, to satisfy a long-standing curiosity. In the first exercise, I experienced what I now know is a "spontaneous initiation," an overwhelming and visceral certainty that THIS IS IT: my *calling*.

Over the next year, as I trained and absorbed everything I could, each and every moment was magical. I made a pilgrimage to Peru to meet my teacher's teachers in the Andes Mountains, and experienced deeper levels of intimacy with Mother Nature and Her beauty. Every ceremony, every method I learned and received opened me to deeper understanding of what it really means to heal: to feel connected to the earth, my own heart, and other people. I discovered what it means to rise up out of words like "victim" and "survivor" and into a new kind of wholeness, independent of the stories we think define us.

There was no way back into a cubicle after all of this.

I launched my website after finishing my apprenticeship and haven't looked back. That's not to say that every moment has been easy. Quite the contrary, actually. Launching my own practice has meant navigating my fears about failure as well as my ideas of success. It continues to mean doing my own internal work so that I show up fully resourced for others. It means I'm not mainstream – and while I wouldn't have it any other way, that distinction has its own challenges. I've seen the doors close in people's eyes when I tell them what I do. I've fielded bizarre questions about animal sacrifice, and even been told outright to "get a real job."

But I won't. I see clients for private healing sessions and facilitate the shifts *they're* craving. I get to help people through *their* fears, illnesses, and dark times. What an extraordinary privilege I've been granted, to be a witness to illumination and insight, and to be part once again of our collective journey into healing. I'm truly blessed to love my work so much and know that it can change lives so profoundly. It truly gets me out of bed in the morning.

Since launching my practice, I've also introduced yoga and shamanism workshops and retreats, spoken publicly, and led ceremonies. I especially enjoy conducting weddings. I wrote and self-published a guide to shifting the energy in the workplace – basically all the things I wish someone had told me when I worked on Wall Street.

The journey for that 23-year-old actress led me through one of the darkest periods of my life. But of course, that's only part of the story. If I hadn't been that starry-eyed ingénue, I would never have worked at the foundation, so that crash course in resiliency and healing would have taken a lot longer. And if I hadn't had PTSD and depression, I might not have this deep well of understanding to source from now, so that I can serve others in their journeys.

Things could not have been any other way, and I am so incredibly grateful to have taken every step.

Mikki Baloy is a shamanic healer and yoga teacher whose approach fuses indigenous traditions with Eastern philosophy and almost three decades of creative training as a performer, writer, and musician. She has been featured in two books about post-disaster resiliency, and now helps soulful people evolve and thrive through ceremony, yoga, and energy medicine. Find out more and read her blog at www.shamanmikki.com.

"Time stood still when I was immersed in building with wood. I found shaping and taming the wood wildly satisfying."

- Patt Gregory

The Song of the Saw

By Patt Gregory

Have you ever listened to the song of the saw?
How it changes its pitch just near the end of the cut?
You don't have to be strong,
It's not like hacking off a branch in the garden,
Sawing is a gentle art...

When I was five I snuck into my stepfather's shed and borrowed his hammer. I spent a few hours wandering around our dairy farm, trying to whack 4-inch nails into the shed door, the laundry window frame and the concrete foundations.

I wanted to build a tree house so I dragged planks of wood up into the wide flowering branches of our wattle tree and tried to nail them to the branches. I then pushed and pulled the less-than-enthusiastic farm dog up onto the couple of wobbly boards I'd wedged in place and together we looked out over the paddocks.

If I had been a boy, I suspect that I would have been shown how to hold the hammer the right way and I would have been told that 4 inch nails have rather limited uses. Instead, when my stepfather discovered I had his hammer, I was sent inside to help Mum with bottling the blackberry jam.

It would be another twenty-seven years before I picked up a hammer again. I was living in the UK and saw a one-line ad in the Bristol Evening Post. It read:

Woodwork for Women – Evening classes – Wed 7 pm – Totterdown – Tel 916743.

I turned up at the terrace cottage and was ushered into a carpeted living room with velour lounges, a TV in the corner and a few small portable workbenches dotted around the space. I was given some fragrant smelling pine, some measuring tools and some instructions to begin to make a slanted desktop writing case. There, in that stuffy lounge room, I had an 'aha' moment – this was what I really wanted to do; I wanted to learn how to build with wood.

The following month I enrolled in an intensive Carpentry and Joinery course. It was twenty-six lads and myself in a classroom at the Bristol Skill Centre. The teacher gave us quick demonstrations and told us to get on with it. It was a 'sink or swim' approach and I certainly did my share of sinking.

I struggled to sharpen my tools as proficiently as the men, couldn't get the hang of keeping my saw straight and upright (required for square and accurate joints), and I always felt like I needed more information but didn't know the right questions to ask.

Despite the frustrations, I loved the spicy wood fragrance as it wafted through the sunlit white workshop. I loved the gleaming sharp tool blades that promised precision and I loved the shooshing sound of the plane as it licked off paper thin, bright golden curls of pine. I was intoxicated by woodwork. Time stood still when I was immersed in building with wood. I found shaping and taming the wood wildly satisfying.

I learned a lot about woodworking in that Bristol classroom but I also learned some important lessons about *how* people learn.

Although the course was about carpentry and joinery, I became aware of how differently I learned the technical elements of the course compared to my fellow male students. I found it was necessary for my tutors to "state the obvious", because I didn't have the basic knowledge of tools and the understanding of terminology that my fellow male students seemed to have.

In 1985, I was fortunate to help set up a Government-funded women's workshop in Bath, UK, and with a group of women, I began teaching woodwork to unemployed women over 25 years of age. This opportunity was an enriching experience indeed, and over a two year period, I helped many trainees to become either teachers themselves or to start their own carpentry business. Some formed their own groups and offered an all-woman service while others found jobs in the industry.

When I returned to my home in Australia and later to a sleepy country town, Mullumbimby, I wondered if the women here would like to learn woodwork, and they did. I set up a pilot course under the government-funded NEIS (New Enterprise Incentive Scheme) and Woodwork for Women was born. It was the awareness of the inequities in technical education that encouraged me to develop a system suited to teaching woodworking to women in an environment of fun and noncompetitiveness, with an emphasis on developing confidence. I designed courses with a holistic approach using mind and body to teach tool handling and the fundamentals of furniture making. My teachings may not follow the conventional route; the students arrive at the end point having gained an understanding of how and why the project is constructed the way it is and how to properly and safely use the tools. I believe that doing endless sample joints until you have acquired the skills to create the perfect joint isn't necessary, so we begin immediately on the actual project.

Women have been coming to courses at my workshop over the past 15 years making furniture - furniture they have designed and made for their homes, such as the daybed, the dining table, bookcases and toys for the kids. Some women have started businesses working with wood and others have been happy to make the rabbit hutch with the kids in the garden on the weekend.

Although I predominantly teach women, it is not exclusive by any means; men have also been coming to my classes over the years and are most welcome. There have been one-on-one classes for children from 4 – 15 years old. Six year-old Felix made his own workbench in hourly lessons once a week after school for several months last year.

I find teaching woodwork is one of the most valuable and rewarding things I have ever done. I love watching faces light up when they hold their finished projects. They glow with confidence at the mention of power tools. They chatter excitedly about their next tool purchase. Women appreciate learning this non-traditional skill with just a small group of other women who share a love of wood and just want to know where to start.

I look forward to travelling next year to teach women how to set up teaching other women and family members how to build with wood.

Patt Gregory has spent much of her working life helping women arm themselves with the knowledge and skills to navigate their way through the timber racks and tool aisles of hardware stores and timber yards. She has inspired hundreds of women to pick up tools, learn woodworking skills and create their own projects.

Woodwork For Women gives women the confidence and skill to work with wood through affordable, fun and practical short courses.
www.woodworkforwomen.com.au

"Forcing myself to think and be positive every single day has taken conscious effort. I have changed what I read, what I watch, what I listen to – everything! – and drown myself in the positive non-stop."
– Su-Mari du Bruyn

It's Okay and You Are Not Alone: Sharing the Challenges of Entrepreneurship

By Su-Mari du Bruyn

Becoming an entrepreneur, although very gratifying, can be very hard. I only knew the corporate world, and making the transition from there to starting and running my own business was much more challenging than I thought. Since then what I have found from engaging with other people who have done or are doing the same thing is that entrepreneurship is very similar to motherhood.

We all go through the same difficulties but we rarely talk about it. New mothers, not understanding what is normal, misunderstand the challenge and difficulty as a signal that they are on the wrong path. With that in mind, if it would help other entrepreneurs going through the same transition, I would love to share with them my story so that they know that it is okay and normal and that they are not alone.

I used to work in a job that was also my life. I worked more than 12 hour days, seven days a week. I gave absolutely everything of myself. I loved my job, cherished the people I worked with, and I did my job very well. Unfortunately, over time things changed until it reached a point where it was clear to me that I would not be able to continue working there until retirement. So I prayed for a sign and when I got it, I resigned without having another job.

I started applying for new positions, but nothing really worked out. It was then one morning that I sat and wondered WHY? I had been obedient to the sign so what was I missing? And then the answers started coming. With a clear vision, I opened my own business with two of my previous colleagues where I now get to positively impact many more organizations and lives.

I feel I am finally living my purpose and I am so grateful for that. Making the transition from being someone in a corporate job to being an entrepreneur is one of the most challenging journeys I have ever undertaken. Forcing myself to think and be positive every single day has taken conscious effort. I have changed what I read, what I watch, what I listen to – everything! – and drowned myself in the positive, non-stop.

From what I have learned on my journey, my advice to new entrepreneurs is that it will probably be more challenging than you imagine and that is perfectly normal.

Your first payday after leaving the corporate world will be hard, but it gets better and it is worth it. You do not know what you do not know – so be willing to learn, learn, learn, learn ALL of the time. If you need to know an answer, don't ever be too afraid to take a chance and ask!

Create a dedicated workspace. Have an action plan in place to prevent yourself from getting lonely. Design a routine for yourself and stick to it. When making your schedule, use the flexibility you have to your advantage.

Stay in a positive space. Have fun and celebrate every achievement no matter how small. The more you enjoy what you are doing, the easier it will be to carry on. This is a simple truth that will help fuel your determination and keep you pushing forward towards greater success.

Su-Mari Du Bruyn is the co-founder of Adapt To Change, headquartered in Parklands, South Africa. She is a qualified HR practitioner and logistics specialist and is passionate about continuous improvement and people development. Through Adapt To Change, she assists businesses to improve their business performance and how to better engage their staff.
www.AdaptToChange.co.za

*"I always knew that when you help and heal others
you help and heal yourself as well."*
- Lena Kennedy

Compelled to Follow my Dreams

By Lena Kennedy

For as long as I can remember "Spirit" has always guided me in my life. Whenever I questioned something, or needed answers or had any doubt about a situation, I would always take time out and delve within and listen to what my spirit was saying. This is your true self, your intuition and that gut feeling that guides you along life's journey.

Although most of my life I have always stepped out on faith, there came a time when I shut down. My passion has always been to teach people about the body; how the body has the ability to heal itself, how powerful the human touch is, that if you can quiet the mind and listen to the body, the healing can begin. I'm not just talking about the physical symptoms but how we can treat them on a more spiritual and mental level before a condition can manifest in the physical body.

As a child, I knew the effect the human touch had. I remember when my mother use to come home from work after standing on her feet all day. I used to get a bucket and soak her feet & massage them for her. I got so much satisfaction in taking care of people and showing them how to take care of themselves. I always knew that when you help and heal others you help and heal yourself as well. There came a time in my life where

I no longer had a passion for healing. I became systemized at a job because the pay was great, but I hated everyday when I had to walk into that place. I suppressed how I felt. I suppressed my passion, my dreams, and my vision, not knowing one day I would be forced to face my divine purpose and destiny through my own experiences.

While I was at work one day, a feeling of resistance came over me and I just didn't want to do it anymore. All of a sudden with that feeling and that thought, my body shut down. I wasn't able to talk and I started to have tremors on my whole right side. Tears were flowing because I didn't know what was happening to me. I was conscious but could not verbalize anything. I was immediately taken to the ER.

After numerous tests, MRIs, and CT scans with everything coming back normal, my condition was diagnosed as "Mystery Illness". After weeks of therapy and still no answers, I went back to what I have taught so many others, which was "quiet the mind and listen to the body". I began to do self-healing, touch therapy and meditation. I incorporated different healing modalities that I had always been passionate about into my own healing.

In the end, I made a full recovery, resigned from my job, packed my bags and went to Thailand where I studied advanced therapeutic bodywork. I then visited Africa where I studied a variety of holistic healing modalities.

I know that illness and healing can both be brought on with a thought and my experience has led me to follow my true divine purpose: to listen to the mind, body, and soul.

My first question that I ask all my clients is: How is your thinking? How are your thoughts? Because this is how we begin to heal.

Lena Kennedy is a Thai bodywork practitioner, the mother of two sons, and owner of Syrebrum Wellness, a naturopathic clinic. Her mission is to inspire and empower people to actively participate in taking control of their health, through natural and holistic means. I view my role in your health as a collaborative one, helping you determine the best steps toward achieving the highest level of wellness possible.
www.lenakennedy.com

"There should be no room for regrets. Celebrate each day with exuberance and intentions."
- Juanita Arrant

Live with Intention

By Juanita Arrant

"The journey of a thousand miles begins with a single step." – Chinese Proverb

From the day I was born, I believed I had loving Christian parents and grandparents, and that I belonged to the Father in Heaven. Things were confusing until I was 17 years of age - then I was spiritually baptized in a lagoon in Hawaii. After that, I felt cherished and bathed in a spiritual love as infinite as the deep blue ocean and as bright as the warmth of the sun. I knew in that instant what my role on earth was.

I had many dreams when I was a young girl and I believed in miracles. I believe they will all come true in time. What favor and blessings I have received!
When my adult life began, I was busy, busy, and still busier! After college, I married my college sweetheart and was soon blessed with a career and jobs I loved. My precious kids were born and I lived for my "*ohana*." They became my world.

With all of the responsibilities in my life – job as a high school teacher, coach, and taking care of everyone's needs – I neglected my inner self and my personal dreams. I had none. But I loved nurturing, caring, mentoring, coaching, and teaching my children and students. I loved making everyone happy and a success! But in the midst of all these experiences, I forgot how to dream my own aspirations and future. When the family and jobs came, my own personal dreams and realizations stopped. WOW! In hindsight, what an eye-opener for me that was.

I had struggled throughout my career as a teacher and coach and I decided not to become an administrator after years of being an instructor. The fears crept in: not enough time for my kids and family, fear or rejections and failures, fear of moving to uncomfortable situations and districts, and risk factors I was not ready to embrace.

God had other intentions for me and these experiences gave me the impetus to charge forward into a brave new world. I started to pursue my purpose and passion in life beyond being a mom or Mrs. A, the coach and teacher.

I discovered that my talents were the differences I'd made with the students and community and I enjoyed making all of those personal contacts. I enjoyed everything about teaching, coaching, mentoring, and working with ALL levels of education – not only with the "at risk" kids and adults, but with the community and my fellow colleagues as well. They were all people and I found that I had many positive and negative experiences – all good for the next stage in my life that God was leading me to.

I have read many books on motivation and inspirations, especially the Bible and my daily devotionals. I continually work on my spirituality and physical alignment to lead a life that is full. Life is a gift. It's an adventure. Every moment is precious and I don't want to waste any time.

I loved learning and increasing my knowledge in everything in life. I loved meeting people both young and old. I enjoyed getting to know them and seeing what makes them smile, laugh, feel good about their lives, and what makes them tick.

There are so many fine folks out there, but how many of us truly want to make new friends and are not afraid to connect and get to know them? It only takes a smile! A friendly and truly good heart will open the door to communications. Age does not matter, gender has no barriers, and positions in life will not keep me from enjoying a new relationship!

Sometimes just a good word to someone could boost his or her morale as well as my own. People love being around positive people. Who wants to hang around a negative person?

I decided this would be my passion – to bring more joy into people's lives. I embrace God's people and serve Him by serving his people. Thus, my business, Nita's Joy, was founded. In my business I serve God and His people. It's not about me – I'm just the vehicle that He speaks through. He guides and directs me and I embrace the adventures.

There should be no room for regrets. Celebrate each day with exuberance and intentions. Live life to the fullest and greet the morning with generosity and yearning to explode with vivaciousness!

No one can make that decision but YOU. No one is in control of your life but YOU. Trust who you are! Surround yourself with positive people and energy!

My husband and I are now empty-nesting and I'm beginning to dream again. It doesn't matter how old or how young you are; anyone can dream again.

You can dream it, achieve it, and live it. Just BELIEVE in yourself!

Nita has over thirty-plus years experience as an educator along with her well-established experience as small business owner. She is strong in faith, is creative, and a classy lady who loves to laugh and have a good time with friends. She has been blessed with a loving family. Her passion and integrity comes through in everything she does, and she can help you become your Highest Self as well.

www.nitasjoy.com

"I relished my new freedom like a newlywed honeymooning on some remote tropical island. The entire world was before me and it was beautiful."

- Lisa Landtroop

Quitting the Corporate Monkey Jungle

By Lisa Landtroop

After almost 20 years in the Corporate Jungle – I quit. Some considered it an act of 'quitting cold turkey.' They, of course, didn't know I'd been planning it for almost two years. My oldest son died in May 2010. By December 2010 the voice perched on my shoulder was whispering into my ear a never-ending mantra of "you're gone too much from home," "your work ethic is telling those closest to you that work is more important to you than they are," and "is this really the example that you want to set? Do you want to continue a legacy of work-a-holics or do you want to lead by example and show your loved ones that there is another way to support your family and also be there for them?"

I began telling my husband throughout most of 2011 that I was seriously thinking of quitting my job and finding a way to make some money by working from home. I was 'greasing the skids,' so to speak to prepare him. He was very supportive, but of course nervous. The act of quitting would mean a different lifestyle for all of us. But many other families survive on just one salary. The real challenge would be whether we would be able to go backwards from the lifestyle we had become accustomed to living.

In January 2011 I wrote a 'quit date' letter to myself. It said I would quit by April of 2012. I spent 2011 absorbing courses, blog posts, and webinars from many of the most highly coveted copywriters, bloggers and entrepreneurs in the world. I absorbed all of the information I could find.

April 2012 came and went and I had not done what I needed to do at home or at work to be in a position to quit. But by May I looked at the calendar and decided that I would quit August 31. I would give my 30 days notice on July 31. My husband accepted the timeline and we began to prepare the household bills for a one salary situation, at least until I could get my own business off of the ground and running. I gave my notice and ended up staying a few weeks longer to help them with the transition. On September 21, 2012 I was a free woman.

For the first time in my adult life I didn't have a job and was able to 'do what I wanted.' The feeling that this freedom brought is indescribable. While I loved my old job, loved what I did and the people I worked with as well as the insanely high-stressed and fast-paced environment of it all, I relished my new freedom like a newlywed honeymooning on some remote tropical island. The entire world was before me and it was beautiful.

I began blogging. I began building an email list. I started ghost copywriting for others and that was my first taste of making money from home. I had finally settled into a routine that gave me an income while letting me work from home on my own terms. I did a plethora of ghost writing, template writing, and other copywriting assignments such as writing other people's web copy for them. My services covered everything from "About" pages to marketing promos, as well as more ghost writing for blogs and articles. I enjoyed the variety – but soon realized I wasn't truly fulfilling my deep desire to help others.

With time, this course that I had begun developing back in February of 2011 started to really take a more solid form and it was time to offer it to the world. It was burning to get out. I launched a self-study version in November of 2012. By early 2013, it was time to offer an instructor-moderated version. I was officially an entrepreneur!

The course is about time awareness and priority management. A course to help you gain control of your schedule and incorporate something back into it each week that you love doing. So many of us tend to work ourselves to death, because we think we are supposed to. We work hard to achieve success and then one day realize that we go weeks and weeks of getting up, going to work, coming home, eating dinner, watching TV, going to bed, and getting up to do it all over again the next day. We don't do anything on the weekends except all of the chores that we didn't have time to do throughout the week because our hours are all taken.

We eventually realize that we haven't done something we enjoy during our 'off hours' in a long, long time. The course helps you figure out where your time thieves are so you can re-incorporate doing something you enjoy into your weekly routine again.

Eventually the course offerings, both the self-study version and the group guided courses with webinars, segued into a coaching model. I was finally able to say that I was working in a profession that allowed me to help people improve their lives, all while working from the comfort of my home. I am able to be home for my family and I wouldn't trade that freedom and flexibility for all the money in the world.

I recognize that most people won't be able to quit without already having some money coming in from their 'side business' and that my position was extremely unique. But the one thing that does ring true no matter your circumstances is that once you decide that you are ready for something more – don't delay, don't let fear hold you back, don't sit and do nothing. Make steps towards your new big dream. Commit to it fully. Even if you do have to work a full-time job during the day and come home and work your new part-time venture at night for a period of time until it grows enough to replace your current salary. Commit.

Lisa Landtroop owns BXLNT (Be eXceLleNT), a multi-platform enterprise specializing in time awareness coaching, copywriting + editing + proofing, & encouraging change leaders. She is the creator of the powerful life-changing course, Take Your Life Back, which helps you remember that life is too short to do stuff you hate! Come on over to Lisa's virtual home located at http://www.TQLTotalQualityLife.com

Part 2: Experiencing a Wake-Up Call

Have you ever experienced a wake-up call? You know, the kind that radically changes how you view the world? You go blindly in life until one day something happens that makes you see it all in a whole new perspective. After your experience, you know nothing can remain as it did before. You have gone through a metamorphosis.

Many of us, when we are younger, follow a path chosen for us. Whether it's influence from our parents, our peers, our teachers, or just society itself, we follow a traditional career trajectory without question. However, when we achieve those conventional goals – nice house, fancy car, and stable career – we often feel empty. We ask ourselves, "Is this all?"

Or perhaps we don't even notice our spirit slowly diminishing as we toil away in jobs that ultimately leave us unsatisfied and unfulfilled. Then BOOM! – a major life event occurs leading to a serious self-evaluation, leaving us questioning the direction our lives have taken, and asking ourselves if it is all worth it.

Each of the stories in this section features a wake-up call that the author experienced propelling her to make a radical life change. One woman shares how a natural disaster in her home state led her to realize life is short and to focus on what was really important. Several other stories mention the deaths of prominent figures in the respective authors' lives, pushing them to make a change.

However, not all wake-up calls are from tragedy. Some are happy discoveries and surprises. One author stumbled upon a hidden artistic talent that became her passion. Another found a love for health and wellness out of her desire to help those she loved around her.

A wake-up call can be anything, really. It's just the spot in time where you can look back and pinpoint where you decided to make a change for the better. What if today was that day? What if a year from now you could look back on today as the day you decided to take the leap and focus on your passion? What would you like to have accomplished in that year?

What would it look like in five years' time? In ten years?

Life is too short to live with a soul unfulfilled. Make today the day you follow your passions and live a life unbound!

"After being an overachieving, extremely self-critical super-performer at my day job for many years, I realized I didn't judge myself when it came to my artwork."

- Chris Blevins

The Passion Hidden Within Me

By Chris Blevins

Never in my wildest dreams did I think I would be an artist. It couldn't have been any farther off my radar screen. I didn't draw or color as a child. I had pretty much zero interest. In fact, I always thought of myself as decidedly un-artistic. I was also quite shy growing up and deathly afraid of public speaking.

Now, at age 55, I am a successful watercolor artist and teacher. My artwork has been featured on wine labels and published in The Artist's Magazine. I teach workshops and host private painting parties. Up until age 48, however, I followed the traditional path of going to college, working for large companies, and climbing the corporate ladder. I had no idea of this artistic talent hidden within.

To this day, I'm not sure exactly why I signed up for that first watercolor class. In hindsight I'd say it was one of those "meant to be" things or "divine providence." I had literally never painted anything other than a wall in my life. I wasn't "crafty," either.

After three tries to sign up for that first watercolor class, I was finally enrolled. It was a series of 10 weekly lessons, and by the third lesson, I was completely enamored, as well as stunned.

I was so enthralled with watercolors I signed up for two weekend workshops while my first series of 10 lessons was still going on! To say I was hooked might be an understatement. That first year I painted over 300 pieces of art.

Not long after my first lesson I received a book, *The Tao of Watercolor* by Jeanne Carbonetti, as a gift. If I thought I was enamored with watercolors before, now I was a complete goner. I had found my style of watercolors: ethereal, fluid, atmospheric, and vividly colored. I was dying to take a class from Jeanne, but she was in Vermont and I was in Washington State. Then I noticed that she was teaching a class in Sedona, Arizona. I thought to myself, "I can do that!" And so I did.

I was newly divorced and went on this trip by myself. Still very much a newbie painter, I dove in anyway. Little did I know this was just a prelude to a bigger adventure. I signed up for Jeanne's private lessons waitlist and a year and a half later, rather than merely flying to Vermont, I paid attention to that little voice in my head and *drove* there. I turned it in to a 10,000-mile, four-week long drive around the United States, by myself. It was a fabulous, life-changing experience.

Not long after beginning to paint, I noticed something really important and very cool. After being an overachieving, extremely self-critical super-performer at my day job for many years, I realized I didn't judge myself when it came to my artwork. Wow. I loved that!

So, I not only found my passion with art, but it led me to teach watercolor classes specializing in students who've never tried painting before. What a delight it is for me, and also for them, as, from what I can tell, I help them find something hiding inside themselves that they had no idea was there. I create a learning environment free from self-criticism. I often refer to "happy accidents" and "flopportunities" in class and just "going with the flow" with whatever happens. This resonates with my spiritual beliefs so I love how this has manifested.

Back at my day job I was feeling more restless, disenchanted, and out of place. The work environment wasn't changing so much, but I sure was. As my interest in art expanded, as well as my spiritual practice, my job dissatisfaction increased. A divine impulsion was going on, and continues to this day. In early 2012, I began in earnest to pursue the art as a livelihood.

On a more positive note, my corporate life equipped me with lots of skills for entrepreneurship. I worked in the finance industry off and on throughout my career. Let me be frank: I don't like working with numbers! I tried many times to get out of the finance department of a company, and would do so, only to somehow land back in finance. At the time it was not funny but now I laugh because all of the stuff I learned about taxes and budgeting and accounting, well, I use all of them to help run my art business!

The other thing I'm particularly grateful for is moving into the training discipline in 1991. This was another one of those "surprises" like art since I was very afraid of public speaking. I ended up really enjoying the training discipline and I've spent many years in the corporate training world, as well as teaching part-time at a local University. I now use all those skills to successfully teach art.

Right before shifting my corporate career into the training discipline, I started to lose my voice. I sounded like I had perpetual laryngitis. After two years of trying to get a diagnosis, and losing my voice to the point of a strangulated whisper, the verdict was in: spasmodic dysphonia, a neurological disorder affecting the vocal cords. I could write a whole story just on that aspect of my life, but suffice it to say, it has been a great teacher and I have not let it stop me. I think it's pretty ironic that I now teach — a lot — and this all began after I started to lose my voice! Interesting how the Universe works!

In January 2012, I set an intention to retire from my day job earlier than full retirement age *and* have enough income from the art to do so. I threw myself into the business end of the art. I invested in a logo, business cards, a website, e-commerce, a Facebook page, record-keeping systems, marketing, etc. I worked hard getting infrastructure and processes set up to save time and allow focus on creating art and building relationships.

Here are two key things I learned from that experience:

1. Hiring, or bartering, for help and not trying to do it all myself was the right thing to do, even though cost concerned me.

2. Following through on leads was imperative.

The most important learning though, has been to let my intuition guide me. It hasn't always been easy, but when I quiet the mind and pay attention, it has been miraculous every time. I'm always surprised when someone tells me how inspirational I am. Then again, I believe that's how we change the world – one person at a time, starting with ourselves, and leading by example.

Here's to the journey!

Chris Blevins plays and paints in Richland, Washington, USA, with her studio dog, Cooper the Schweenie. For some vibrant watercolor eye candy, visit her website at www.chrisblevinswatercolors.com.

"I love my job and I love my company. They have changed my life and the lives of my loved ones. I found the biggest passion I ever thought I could have!"

- Gretel Lindbloom

Mi Historia

By Gretel Lindbloom

My name is Gretel Lindbloom. I am a Mexican woman who is passionate about health. I am currently living in the USA, a completely different culture from the one in which I grew up.

There are three important people in my life that inspired me to do what I'm doing now. One of them is my dad. He left his parents' house at 14 years old. He knew what he wanted in life and moved to Mexico City to be with relatives that had all of the things he wanted. He worked hard doing all kind of things no matter how hard they were. He had a dream in mind and made it happen. He owned his own business for 40 years and kept it growing the whole time.

Nowadays, he has the freedom and money to enjoy his second passion: driving motorcycles all over the place. He is also a health nut like me. He is proof that a balanced life style will keep you strong and healthy. He does not take any medication at 68 years of age. He is the perfect example of determination, strong work ethic, and dreaming big combined, and taking action to make his dreams come true.

The second person that inspires me is my mother. She was diagnosed with multiple sclerosis in 2008. She was in pain for years but was misdiagnosed. She always fought the pain and tried everything to feel better. She never stayed home and cried, she didn't even tell us how bad her condition was. No one knew her real situation. I thought she was simply depressed.

The doctor told her there was no future for her. She could not drive by herself and was confined to a wheel chair and bed. There where no hopes or any kind of solutions. Despite her pain she still volunteered with her church everyday helping in different places and some times she would drive up to one hour from home. With her hurt leg, she put herself in danger but she did not say anything and kept driving for years.

The same year she finally got a correct diagnosis, I had been sick as a dog for almost two years with allergies and sinus troubles. Never in my life had I experienced such a reaction to the place I was living. I was feeling sick every day. I took medication that made me feel so sleepy that even the next day I couldn't function properly. Because my kids were little and needed me, and the medicine did not clear my symptoms, I felt there was no point in taking it. I was told by a friend of mine about a natural solution to fix my allergies, but I did not listen to her. I completely closed my mind to any kind of possible options for me. I told myself she was just a salesperson. I went to the doctor and told her the medicine didn't work for me.

I also had troubles with my digestion. I went to another doctor and had a colonoscopy but he did not give me any explanation regarding my problems. Instead he told me, "You are fine. Broccoli cause gas and inflammation."

It is so frustrating to leave a doctor's office feeling so hopeless.

When my parents came to visit, my mother was desperate to find help for her health condition. It took her three times to ask me to call my friend. Even looking at her on the floor many times resting, I was blind. It was a surprise that we found a solution and a way to keep my mother moving. Slowly, she got better.

We live in a fast world. We want a fix now. We don't want to wait. We want the pill that will kill the pain. In wellness, the journey can be longer but more stable and truly healing. Seeing my mother's path to wellness, I became inspired to heal and help others become well.

My friend gave me the idea of what to do and the rest is history. I started reading everything related to digestion. I learned a lot and discovered what food intolerances were and what they do to people. I fell in love with learning how my body works and how all of the systems in my body are like one big team.

I changed my diet and went back to my old roots of eating fresh food. I had let myself go for a while and suffered a severe acne attack. I felt like I was going through puberty one more time. I did a food allergy test to figure out what was causing my problems. What a surprise – I was eating a lot of good food that my body had problems with. I took probiotics and enzymes again and my face started clearing. These bacteria are necessary for our overall health and should be part of our daily regiment. I learned that on my own. I also learned that the birth control pills I took for many years affected the gut flora like antibiotics do, and were one of the reasons for my digestion problems.

My daughter also inspires me. She had horrible tonsillitis as a kid and had to have her tonsils removed. She had focus problems at school and the school just wanted to treat her as slow learner. She developed allergies that got worse every year as well as asthma. She would have asthma attacks just sitting at home doing nothing.

I helped her with the same line of products that had helped me, and had her tested for food allergies. She had been allergic to eggs, gluten, wheat, yeast, and more. These foods were part of her regular diet and were damaging her Gastro-Intestinal digestive tract and creating inflammation in her respiratory system.

She feels much better now. She is a very responsible kid that works hard and gets good grades in school. NO more medications for her – only antioxidants, B vitamin complex, probiotics, and vitamin D. They have made a huge difference, and knowing the reason for her health problems changed everything. If I had followed my regular doctor's protocol, my daughter would be full of steroids, damaging her even more. If I had closed my mind she probably would have lost her confidence as a student and potentially her credibility of being a responsible adult with dreams and goals. She keeps playing soccer, basketball, and running. She is free of steroids. This is an amazing feeling!

I have learned that nowadays it is hard to find an honest company that makes products that actually work and that our body can utilize. Our body does not always absorb and make use of whatever we eat. It is more complex than that. A lot of people have a damaged digestion system and unbalanced bacteria. I believe it is one of the reasons why there are many autoimmune diseases and mental illnesses.

I love to learn everyday and help others. We can't leave our health in other people's hands. If we do, we can lose the opportunity to heal. My mother didn't listen to the doctor and she is here, alive and moving, and still volunteering with her church. The best part is that she can travel and visit her granddaughters in the USA. I love to help people find solutions. When I see them, and they are feeling better, I get a big smile, hugs, and a thank you. Those things make me feel super special.

I love my job and I love my company. They have changed my life and the lives of my loved ones. I found the biggest passion I ever thought I could have!

Gretel Lindbloom went to school in Mexico and earned a degree in communication sciences. She is married with two children and resides in Portland, Oregon. After being a stay-at-home mom for many years, she now helps people to get healthier in a more natural way as a Nutraceutical representative.
www.isotonix.marketamerica.com/lindbloom

"While not gone, my gypsy gene was sedated by the normalcy of a regular life and what I thought I 'should' be doing. And I was completely miserable."

- Haley Hines

Filling My Gypsy Spirit

By Haley Hines

There have been two times in my life where I was required to be really brave.

Here is my story:

I think I've always had the "gypsy" gene. It is a certain trait I could not explain that ignited my imagination, showed up in my dreams, and tugged at my heart. This might be considered a positive and liberating trait in some cases, but while I really wanted to join the Peace Corps or travel and discover magical places in the world, everyone I knew was getting married and settling down. So instead of running off, I signed up for what was considered the "normal" and "appropriate" way to live life. Before I knew it, I was married, had a house with a white picket fence, and living what most people would consider the American Dream, all by my mid-20s. While not gone, my gypsy gene was sedated by the normalcy of a regular life and what I thought I "should" be doing. And I was completely miserable.

Fast-forward seven years. Even with my best efforts, my marriage was a disaster. I'd created a life that looked nothing like me, and I looked in the mirror one day and didn't even recognize myself. No sparkle, no razzle-dazzle left. I realized I had a huge decision to make: live this way the rest of my life or leave. I decided to leave, and it was the single best decision I ever made. Scary? Yes. Easy? Not even a little bit. I had to start completely over but it was so worth it. I started to rebuild and create exactly what I wanted my life to be.

Starting Over

Having always been entrepreneurial, I started my lifestyle design company, La Bella Living. I was left with quite a bit of debt from my divorce and struggled to really thrive on my own. I began consulting with a corporate wellness company in Dallas, which quickly grew to full time. When an opportunity arose to join a large benefits firm to drive their corporate wellness strategies, I thought I had achieved the freedom I was so desperately seeking. While some financial independence was comforting, my corporate life still didn't seem to fit me.

For another eight years, I continued to suppress my gypsy urges and rose up the corporate ladder, first achieving success at the large benefits firm, and then moving back to the wellness company as an executive reporting to the CEO. This was my "dream job." While

The corporate environment was financially rewarding, I could not shake the nagging feeling that there was still more work in the world that I needed to be doing. I needed to make a change. The problem was after years without any payments, I had purchased a house and then a car. This was me trying to be responsible.

"Grown-ups have things," I told myself. "Like mortgages and car payments."

Although I really wanted to run with my gypsy plan, I was scared to let go of the security I had. To help appease my renegade side, I began to scope out what my life would look like if I was able to escape the inertia of my normal life. I called my plan "Operation Gypsy", and set a framework that would help guide my dreams.

All I needed was a push.

Life is Short

That push came on May 20th after a tornado hit Moore, Oklahoma, the town I grew up in. Listening to the news helplessly from my home in Dallas, there was a 42-minute window when I could not get in touch with anyone in my family. Seeing my childhood friends carry their children away from unrecognizable elementary schools and hearing story after story of friends that had lost everything brought me the clarity and perspective I needed. I thought about what was important to me, how quickly things can change, how my heart wasn't truly happy, and how life is really short. Then it hit me: what on earth am I waiting for?

I had already rented out my house and paid off my car, and had been saving as much as possible, so I resigned from my job. And yes, it was scary! I left the security, the paycheck, the stability, fancy title, great people and lovely office to explore the next chapter. It was time for a new season and my opportunity to do what I was born to do – inspire, motivate, educate, and love people so they can find their path to healthy living and healthy loving.

Dreams Come True

Operation Gypsy was on! I re-launched my company, La Bella Living - a dream I've had for years. I am taking my show on the road and designing products and services that help people create a life they love. I help them find passion and purpose and provide a way for them to do more of what they were born to do. I am creating a business model that allows me to cultivate my own dreams and aspirations and create income streams that allow me to work anywhere around the world so I can travel. The first project I'll be partnering with is the Africa Yoga Project, allowing me to travel to Kenya in early 2014 to support the amazing programs they are offering in Nairobi.

The most important thing for me in making this decision was the unshaken belief that I can make this work. I can follow this path and do what may appear to be crazy to some but not be afraid to do it anyway. I am giving myself permission to follow my heart and do my life's work – my soul's work. It is important to me to live and love with my whole heart and not have any regrets.

Bestselling author Brené Brown refers to what happens at midlife not as "a crisis" but as an unraveling. She describes it as a desperate pull to live the life you want to live, not the one you are "supposed" to live. It's the time when you are challenged by the universe to let go of who you think you are supposed to be and to embrace who you are.

Life is too short to do what we think we "should" do instead of doing the work our heart longs for. Believe in the vision you have for the life you want to live. Surround yourself with people that are supportive of your dreams and encourage you to pursue them. Find a community of people that are on the same path and spend time with them. Use vision boards to visualize your desires – they are a powerful way to bring your dreams to reality.

I had consulted with hundreds of employers implementing health management programs and creating new innovative product offerings for fifteen years before I left the corporate world to follow my heart and focus on my loves. I wanted freedom, deep connection, meaningful conversations, and impactful work.

Creating my own path and definition of success has been exciting and crazy all at the same time. I have realized we don't have to be defined by a role or a title; we can be a bit of everything that lights us up. I am ready to put my passion into action and make an impact.

Leave a legacy, create change.

It's really scary, but it also feels very brave.

"If your heart is yearning for something, it is your duty to find the courage to listen, then take action. Not just for you, but for all of us." - Nisha Moodley

Hayley Hines draws from more than a decade and a half of experience gained from exploring wellness and health in both public and private sectors. Hayley is an accomplished speaker and a Certified Health Education Specialist. She has an extensive educational background in Nutrition (Bachelor of Science, University of Texas) and Health Promotion Management (Masters of Science). She is a graduate of the Institute for Integrative Nutrition and a 200 Hour Registered Yoga Teacher. Her passion is to help individuals, families, and companies create and maintain a healthy culture.

http://labellaliving.com/

"I was the person who switched jobs every two years all the while thinking that I would be happier in a better position. I never was."
- Jeannie Spiro

Beyond the 9 to 5: How I Became a Moonlighting Entrepreneur

By Jeannie Spiro

After college graduation, I accepted the first corporate job that would pay my bills. It was a good company with great benefits and potential to rapidly climb the corporate ladder. The only problem was that wasn't the path I wanted to take.

Early in my senior year of college, I finally decided what I wanted to be when I grew up – a teacher. Because it was too late to change majors, I accepted my fate and my Speech Communication degree and headed into the world of corporate health insurance.

Playing the game was expected. I dressed the part, worked long hours and by my early thirties was managing a team of ten staff members. But I wasn't happy.

I was the person who switched jobs every two years all the while thinking that I would be happier in a better position. I never was.

With kids came more pressure to earn more and work harder. So I began working longer hours, traveled more and found myself overcompensating for not being home with them. I began to unravel. The stress was mounting, the coffee intake was rising, and sleep barely happened.

Then the unthinkable happened. One day at work, my boss and mentor collapsed and died of a heart attack. I was heartbroken and suddenly painfully aware that my life was headed in the same direction. Within weeks, I quit my job, cut my salary in half and took a part time position. That's when my reinvention began.

With more free time and my priorities in order I began to explore how I could marry my love of teaching with my many years in the corporate world. That's when I discovered coaching.

Having a multiple page resume of skills was only so helpful when it came to starting a business but I didn't let it stop me; I dove in to learn everything I could and hired mentors to help me with what I couldn't learn on my own.

But there were a few problems. I still didn't have a niche and because I didn't have enough clients, I couldn't leave my job.

That's when it hit me: in order to get clients, I needed to leverage the Internet in the tiny pockets of time I had. Once I knew how to create consistent revenue I would be able to quit my job and work in my business full time. So I set out to learn all that I could to work productively, master the Internet, and create multiple streams of consistent income.

It was then that my niche came alive in front of me and my business began to blossom. The very process I created for myself became the specialization I would teach over and over again. My mission became helping other women create a freedom and passion-based business online so they could leave their 9 to 5 job behind.

I'm proud to say that I've rapidly grown my coaching business, crossed the Internet, work with clients in multiple countries, and have established myself as an expert in my field.

I've taken the very process I followed and have created a program where I help other women discover how to make the leap to entrepreneurship with a solid foundation of clients and revenue in place.

All my years in the corporate world have served me well but nothing compares to having a freedom and passion-based business.

Jeannie Spiro is an Online Business & Marketing Strategist helping women all over the world grow their business online. After a long corporate career in sales and marketing, Jeannie started her coaching business and quickly found that the key to success was to grow her business online.

Jeannie helps women strategically grow their business and create a 6-figure freedom based business plan. You can learn more about her and her services at http://jeanniespiro.com/

"One of the things I have learned is, 'Leap and the world will throw you a net.'"
- Sara James Williams

Seeing My Life with My Own Eyes

By Sara James Williams

A year ago, big wake up calls started happening, calling for me to leap.

This is why and how it happened.

Last summer my daughter attempted suicide and it scared me into submission and weakness. I remember her saying I was no help to her and to leave her alone. It terrified me and mirrored a past I was certain I had left behind. The universe will keep delivering your secrets to you until you release them and they are no longer secrets anymore.

When I was a young teenager, I watched as my once loving step-mom turned into the most psychotic person I have ever met before or since. Her suicide attempts were numerous and usually were blamed on me. When this identical situation appeared in my daughter, I was frightened. I couldn't believe how my past rushed in, and I crumbled into a 13-year-old girl reliving the entire trauma.

I recall telling my boss this had happened and she gave me permission to take the day off. I declined because I believed I wasn't wanted or needed. I remember being aware that something about my numb reaction was wrong.

Contributing to this eventual wake up call was a new coworker. He had a relationship with a client my company desperately wanted but held a victim mentality. He perceived anything anyone said to him as criticism and he responded as such. He managed his victimhood by bringing everyone else down with him. He was very difficult to work with.

I took daily harassment from him for four months. I reported it to the Human Resources department, my manager, and his manager several times, and I was promised many changes. However, the situation only got worse. My last email to him read, "I'm totally done taking any and all of your passive aggressive crap, now or ever again." Suddenly management was listening and a meeting was scheduled the following week for conflict resolution.

Right in the middle of all of this mess, I got my final wakeup call:

My Dad had died.

I remember crying until it physically hurt, and feeling lost, alone and broken. I sat with my step-mom, my uncle, and all of the friends he made. I listened to the Medical Examiner say weird things like, "You'll need to call the funeral home to retrieve his body." What funeral home? What the #@$! are you talking about? I was completely bewildered.

I took the three allowed bereavement days from work but I started working immediately – just not at my actual job. I am a project manager, so organizing and planning is what I do. I was doing it now for my step-mom because at the moment, I perceived I was the stronger of the two of us.

My Dad was the light in my life, my whole life. He was the risk-taker – the do-what-you-need-to-do-to-be-happy person. He lived out loud and loudly. His laugh was infectious. Some would say he had nothing – no life insurance, little money, lived in a single-wide trailer and had a broken Harley Davidson.

But this is how I see it: He died a **very** wealthy man. He had dozens of friends that he called family and great family that has stepped in to love each other in the midst of this craziness. He always had enough money to do the things he wanted to do. He loved his beautiful custom Harley. Broken, not broken, didn't matter.

And he loved me completely.

My response to his death was to swoop in, take care of the logistics, and return to work.

Weeks before, I had committed to going to my friend's transformational event in Los Angeles. To date, it was the best thing I have ever done for myself. Halfway through the weekend, my husband and I drove out to the Santa Monica Pier to play and enjoy time together. Instead, I stood on the pier crying while my helpless husband tried to help me.

"What can I do? What do you need? How can I help?"

I told him I needed to leave, and stormed off the pier and out to the beach where the sand was wet and sat down. I sat there and cried and observed these thoughts for an hour:

"I have to quit my job. I almost lost my daughter, I hate my job and I lost my Dad!"
"You have bills and child support to pay! What are you going to do?"
"I'm going to write a book and tell my story."
"You are lost and alone."
"I wonder what my husband's visualization house looked like?"

At that moment I heard him say, "We should go back to the hotel." I stood up and he had been standing behind me the whole time! Voice shaking, I said, "I have to quit my job." And he said, "Okay." Then I asked him "What did your visualization house look like?" "It was on the island, shaded in Madrona trees. No yard out front with a red door and a giant shop for me to woodwork." It looked **exactly** like my house! I was connected again!!

When I got back to my room that night, I texted Kyle, the leader of the event I was attending, and told him, "I realized I have been judging myself through other people all my life. I'm quitting my job to write and tell my story. I blame you and thank you from the depths of my soul."

To close out the weekend, Kyle invited me onstage to share what happened on the beach the night before and the wakeup calls before that. To my astonishment, the audience was crying with me and on their feet applauding me!

Everything that happened after that was a whirlwind of greatness! I received job offers, a publisher possibility for my book and podcast invitations – all to tell my story. All of this amazing stuff was happening and I still needed to give notice at work.

I could've told my boss I was sick or had the flu and instead approached her with honesty. I told her I wasn't coming in that week, that I was okay, and would share details as soon as I had them. I expected one phone call or email. I got eight phone calls and emails demanding that I reveal why I wasn't at work. If I had lied, this wouldn't have happened, but I offered up some truth and felt they couldn't handle it.

I flew home a few days later and I awoke my first morning home with the words to share with my boss. I typed up an email thanking her for everything she did for me. I did not just say those words; I gave her details of the exact gifts she bestowed upon me as my manager for five and a half years.

And then I quit.

I am a human being and am only owned by myself. Whatever the consequences are, I accept them. Every day is a new gift! I write, meditate and laugh every day.

One of the things I have learned is, "Leap and the world will throw you a net."

I have leapt and the net showed up!

Sara James Williams is a 35-year-old mother, wife, daughter, and sister. She is on a truth-seeking journey both internally and externally and enjoying every minute the world has to offer her. She and her daughter are closer now than they have been in years, and are thankful for all of the moments they have together. She lives north of the Seattle area with her husband and their two dogs. Sara and her husband are currently planning to sell their home

and buy their dream property in the San Juan Islands.
www.sarajameswilliams.com

"It's not easy, but it's worth it, my friends! I only wish I had made some of my changes earlier in life."
- Shari Yantes

Changing My Focus

By Shari Yantes

Today I'm finally living my dream and supporting myself as an Author, Speaker, Facilitator and Personal Development Coach. Not only am I living the dream in my professional life, but I've also made significant changes in my personal life to be living authentically there as well!

I feel very fortunate to have finally made changes I knew I wanted to make many years ago, but didn't for a variety of reasons: doubt, fear, shame, others' expectations, and potential embarrassment.

I grew up in a small rural town in Minnesota the size of approximately 300 people. I always felt like I was "different" – not better or worse than anyone else, just different. I had lots of friends from a variety of backgrounds and very supportive parents, but I never really felt like I found my place.

My mother has been my rock for years. My parents divorced when I was 15 years-old. My biological father was a successful entrepreneur and alcoholic who died an early death at the age of 51 from cancer. He was a work-hard, play-hard kind of guy. My stepfather passed away in 2011 at the early age of 65. He was a recovering alcoholic and had been sober for almost 25 years at the time of his death. My parents have all been a huge influence on my life and have supported me in everything I've done – teaching me I can do, and be, anything I want.

I have one brother – my biggest supporter and closest friend – and four stepsisters, including one who died an early death, partially contributed to her unfortunate chemical addiction. I have a daughter who was born in 1992 and a son born in 2003; the first was a "planned" pregnancy, and the second was a very large, but wonderful surprise!

I have been married and divorced twice; the first divorce was not amicable, while the second was, and my second husband and I remain friends today. I have survived physically and mentally abusive relationships, but more importantly, I have thrived in spite *or* because of them! In all of my romantic relationships, I felt something was missing. I never felt comfortable and still had that feeling that I hadn't found my place in life.

After school, not knowing exactly what I wanted to do, I accepted a secretarial position near my hometown. After working there a couple of years, I decided I wanted to move to the city in my early 20s. Small town Minnesota wasn't for me. I was still feeling like I hadn't found my place and I wanted "more". Moving from a town of 300 people to an apartment complex that housed more than that was a huge adjustment – but one I loved!

I entered corporate America and quickly began to work my way up. I spent the next 20+ years leading Human Resources departments in both Fortune 100 companies as well as family-owned businesses. I received the most inspiration and happiness from helping others succeed and follow their dreams, so I knew I needed to leave the corporate world to devote myself to helping people find authentic happiness and success.

What finally gave me the strength to make the changes? My stepfather became ill and was forced to give up the entrepreneurial life he had been leading. This was very hard for him; however, as a veteran, he quickly became active with the Veteran's Association. I watched his joy of volunteering and helping others even though he was quite ill. My mom became a caretaker and gave up things that brought her joy. I spent a lot of time living in what is sometimes referred to as the "sandwich generation" where I was taking care of my parents and my kids.

My stepfather passed away in March, a stepsister passed away in August, and my "little sister" (stepsister) got married in October all in the same year. My marriage was very platonic. We were sleeping in different rooms and treated each other more as roommates than spouses so we decided to end our marriage. I had a teenage daughter that was making some poor decisions and I had a young son who began commenting on the lack of "family". I also had a job that was more focused on the corporate dollar than the employee's wellbeing, which caused integrity concerns for me at work.

With all of these major life changes in one year, the shift began. Losing two fathers and a stepsister at early ages in their life and going through another divorce, it was like a slap in the face telling me that life is too short to be unhappy. When I realized how happy I could be, I changed my focus to the good things in my life and catapulted forward. I met a person that I adored and fell in love with quickly. It was a non-traditional relationship but I had finally found what was missing in all of my relationships!

The best advice I can give you is to focus on what makes you happy and what is working rather than focusing on the negative. What you focus on is what happens in your life. Listen to your body; your feelings are your best indicators of what is working for you and what isn't. If it doesn't feel good to you, don't do it. Move on.

Fear, doubt, shame, feeling like you might let someone else down are all things that are hard to overcome, but you must put yourself first. If you are not your authentic true self, you can't help others be theirs! There will be people who judge you, people who get upset with you, and people who are just plain jealous of you when you make changes. You may also lose some connections depending on the changes you make.

HOWEVER: You'll be a better person. You'll be happy, more confident, and probably more successful. The people who really love you for who you are will still be by your side and you'll make new connections with like-minded people.

It's not easy, but it's worth it, my friends! I only wish I had made some of my changes earlier in life.

Now it's time for you to go out there and live your dream!

Shari is an author and Personal Success Coach who has been coaching, mentoring, speaking and training for 20+ years. She spent many years in corporate America, with both Fortune 100 companies as well as family-owned businesses, leading Human Resources departments. Finding the most inspiration and happiness in helping others succeed and follow their dreams, Shari left the corporate world and devoted herself to helping people live their dreams and find authentic happiness and success.

Shari is available to help you be your true self and find your way to an authentic thriving life. Please visit her at www.shariyantes.com.

Part 3: Drive to Fulfill Purpose

Do you feel a tugging in your heart leading you to a certain passion? Is there something in your life that you enjoy so much that you feel complete bliss when you are engaged in it? Do people often tell you that you should be in a certain profession due to a natural talent or skill?

Many people state that they feel "called" to a certain trade or occupation. They experience a burning down deep inside that causes them emotional pain when they deny it. When asked why they chose a certain path in life, it seems ridiculous (impossible?) to them that it would be any other way.

When you are working towards your life's purpose, you know it. You feel it in your heart and in your soul. You feel it all over. We begin using our talents and visions to help others achieve theirs. Even though you may not know where you are going, you know you are heading in the right direction.

The authors of this next section all felt a calling deep inside their souls urging them to follow their unique life paths. Even when already in an adequate occupation, these women felt compelled to do something different.

They had a desire to live life by their heart and give something positive back to the world.

Finding one's life purpose doesn't always come easily. Many people end up waiting for fate or destiny to show them the way, but that isn't how it usually happens. You must be proactive. To have a purpose in life, you must live purposely. Go out and create your own meaning by finding something that you enjoy doing and do it.

What is it that you always wanted to do? What unique skills and talents can you employ to positively impact the lives of those around you? How can you make the world a better place?

Have courage to act as your spirit directs, find your life's purpose, and live a life unbound!

"Look at this! Look at you all! I came to America from Belgium, just me and my wife, and look at what I built. Look at my family."
- Kerry Swetmon's 100-year-old grandfather, Julien.

The Line in the Sand

By Kerry Swetmon

When I was a little girl, my greatest desire was to be a mom and also to be just like my Great Grandpa Julien. Truly. All I really wanted was to love my babies, be a wife, and live a really long, happy life like Jules. I remember really grasping for straws when people asked me what I wanted to be.

Somehow I knew I was supposed to pick a career as my answer, not motherhood. So, when it came time to choose a major in college, I totally floundered. First, Liberal Arts, which is pretty much what students choose when you have no clue what path to choose. Then I chose Food Science because of my love for cooking (and the lack of a culinary program at the University of Florida).

This path didn't last long as I quickly realized anything with the word "Science" in it was not going to work out well for me. It was down to the wire and I really couldn't continue my schooling without selecting a major. What to do? The decision was finally made based simply on the major that I had the most college credit towards: Business Management.

And even though the stars were secretly aligning, I had no idea what I would do with a Business Degree. I vividly remember my dad saying, "So, what'd you pick?"
"Business," I replied.
"Business? What are you going to do with that?"
"Hmphf," I thought, "Hell if I know!"

Toward the end of college, I really started to enjoy my classes. I particularly liked Human Resources and Operations. At a career fair, I was recruited as a Management Trainee for a fairly large corporation in Atlanta, Georgia. The company had a very strong recruiting officer who enticed me with a beautiful brochure listing all the various career paths. They offered me a whopping $29K salary and I was on my way! I moved 7 hours from my hometown to a strange city to begin a new chapter in my life.

Upon arriving at my new J-O-B, I had my mind set on the position of Controller. It seemed to encompass all of the things I learned (and enjoyed) in college. Yet, when I arrived in Atlanta, there was someone in that position. What? I learned very quickly that "Management Trainee" really meant I would work in Sales in a showroom where all the other pretty young girls worked. And, as it turned out that $29K was hourly, and unless I worked 7-7 Monday – Friday, I wouldn't earn even that!

I felt like a real jackass. Swindled. Taken. Undermined. But, I'm a team player, and I decided to make a "go" of it. I would just work hard to get where I wanted, right? After all, that's what my Great Grandpa did. Julien and his wife, Maria (whom I never met) moved to America from Belgium in 1922. They arrived through Ellis Island, and their ship's manifest documented Julien as a weaver and his native language as Flemish. I can still picture him sitting in his rocker in my grandmother's house, thumping his two fingers on the arm of the chair. I loved to sit in his lap and stare out the window.

Anyway, this company for which I was now working sent all the new recruits to its headquarters for a little gathering and training within the first year of employment. I remember receiving the email with my particular travel plans for going to headquarters. There was a trainee in the office who had just returned so, in conversation, I asked, "What did you wear while at headquarters?"
She said, "Just wear what you wear to work – business attire."
Got it.

But, unbeknownst to me, I would come to regret not reading the email thoroughly. On the 2nd day at headquarters, I was pulled aside by the same gal that recruited me to the company and she said,
"What's going on?"
"Not much," I replied (completely oblivious), "This is great!"
"Don't you have anything else to wear?"
I'm thinking, oh crap, what's on me? Have I peed myself? Sat in something? Is the toilet paper sticking out of my pants? What could it be?
"No. Why?," I ask.
"Women aren't allowed to wear pants at headquarters."

WHAT?
Did she seriously just say something straight out of Leave It To Beaver? Surely I'm in the twilight zone, right? "What year is it?" I think in a panic. It's 2001 – I'm sure of it.

I say to the recruiter, "Not allowed to wear pants? You're joking, right? I am wearing a suit. I'm not allowed to wear a PANT-suit?"
Her smile turned sour and the response was,
"No, it was in the email. Our President does now allow women to wear pants at headquarters. If I were you, I'd sit down and not move."

For the moment, this was fine for me because I couldn't move – I literally couldn't believe my frickin' ears. Not allowed to wear a professional suit that happened to have pants in lieu of a skirt? As you might imagine, this was the beginning of the end for me at this company. I spent the remaining hours thinking of snarky comments about this newfound ridiculousness. If I hadn't been 600 miles from home, I would've left right then. But I was in shock, I think. And, honestly, this crushed me. How did I end up here?

I learned a lot from that experience. We worked with VERY high-end clients in the showroom and it was a great lesson in being non-judgmental with sales conversations. Watching women spend $600 on a toilet paper holder was eye-opening to say the least. It became obvious that I should never assume anything about a potential customer.

I also learned to trust my gut instinct. In looking back, I knew, deep down, something was fishy before I accepted that job offer, yet I allowed myself to ignore it. Finally, I learned that selling out my Soul to "succeed" was NOT an option. I always worked really hard at everything I did and although there was some sense of failure when I considered quitting, the Truth in my heart was louder than that small sense of failure. I couldn't work 7-7 doing something I didn't love. And I really tried to love it.

Having said all that, the most important outcome of that job (as fate would have it) was meeting my husband just a few months before I quit. He came into the showroom to purchase some material for a client. I now know, of course, that this was the biggest reason I worked there. My husband was, and is, a successful entrepreneur. He's not been without his own trials in business but, in true entrepreneurial style, he just keeps going.

In the years following that showroom job, I became a Small Business Strategist. I, quite coincidentally, met different small business owners who needed help. Armed with my degree, some natural talents, and my work history, I had ideas, strategies and knowledge to help them. With each small business, I rolled up my sleeves and dug in, studying systems and establishing new ones – a small business makeover of sorts. Even at my very first job at merely 15 years old working at a candy store in the mall, I immediately took the reins and was opening and closing the store by myself and establishing systems within the first few months. In looking back, I was always an entrepreneur, but one without a business.

I spent the next several years being the entrepreneur with no business. Somewhere along the line, it had been impressed upon me that I would be a corporate ladder climber, not an entrepreneur! I didn't even question that. It was just something I knew until everything started to fall apart.

Around 2006 when the economy seemed to be doing a nosedive into a fiery recess, my husband's business started to suffer. This became what would be one of the biggest turning points in my life. We lost everything, even each other for a bit. We had to liquidate a million dollars in real estate and found ourselves in dire straits with two small children facing a completely unknown future.

To say it was rough is a gross understatement. At thirty years old, I found myself suddenly reaching out to my parents for backup. And thank the Good Lord for them because it's hard to think about what would've happened without their support.

My husband went through a period of "shut-down." His business had always done very, very well and with everyone and their mothers now calling for money we didn't have, he literally sunk into a deep, horrifying depression. Like I said, it was the worst time of my life. Quite suddenly, I went from living this really comfortable, luxurious lifestyle to feeling ignorant and living a life riddled with anxiety, unknowing, and fear.

This was the turning point. This was the point at which I drew a line in the sand. I knew one thing at that time and one thing alone: I'll be damned if this ever happens again. NO WAY would I find myself in that situation again. Is it possible it could happen again? Anything is possible, but I am now armed with knowledge and experience. I can't (and won't) forget what I learned. And so it was! My first business was born.

Ironically, fifteen years of being in business didn't guarantee my own success at owning a small business. Not even close! The first official business I started was a pipe company – as in cast iron pipe. Weird? Pretty much! Without going into too much detail, I started the business because I saw a way to make money. Or, at least, I THOUGHT I saw a way to make money. Apparently, not so much! Through a series of obstacles and big red flashing lights, I tried and tried to get that thing off the ground. It didn't work. The business was created out of desperation and panic. I didn't have a "why" or a passion. In looking back, I realize that the pipe company never stood a chance.

A few years later, I started another business, an e-commerce store. This business is successful and I'm very proud of it, but I still felt as though something was missing. I knew I was meant for more. I had been listening to other women (in various networking groups) say they "felt compelled" to do their work. I thought, "I surely do not feel compelled to sell handbags and jewelry!" (not that I don't believe there are people who are gifted to do just that.) What was wrong with me? I was distraught and couldn't understand how I could lead so many other small businesses from stagnant or failing to thriving yet continue to feel frustrated in my own business.

Fortunately, after 3 years of struggle, my husband was "back in the saddle," and his new business was skyrocketing. It gave me the added push, the "why the Hell not me?" I began a deep and spiritual exploration. I asked a lot of questions and surrounded myself with like-minded women entrepreneurs. And in that process, an idea evolved.

Although it felt magical, this idea was right on the end of my nose. I just couldn't see it. Helping small businesses is my purpose. It's what provides me true fulfillment. And, as long as I listen to that inner guidance, my entire life (and income) continues to improve. My exploration revealed that if I was going to be an entrepreneur and live my purpose, I needed to own a business that helped small businesses!

I remember feeling as though the heavens parted when I figured this out. I was so happy and encouraged. But shortly thereafter, I began thinking, "Ok, so, now what?" What am I going to do with this knowledge? And, yet again, I launched a campaign within myself to find answers. The evolution continued.

This is what I know: You must use your business as an expression of yourself.

Whatever that means for you, I know this is the key to gaining freedom and money. The more you truly comprehend, nurture, and connect to your true, greatest Self, the more easily you achieve your true, greatest purpose. This is the mission of Life•Business•Growth (LBG), my third business.

LBG was born out of my heartache for women with the passion and purpose to change the world yet are unable to be seen and heard. These women are on the same journey of spiritual awakening as I am. They just want to make money owning a business and doing what they love so as to nurture their Soul and live a life full of rich experiences and relationships.

LBG evolved from my heart. I knew I could help these women change the world by giving them a platform on which to reach their audience and teach their message. I also knew that if I could encourage other women to embrace the intertwined path of spiritual AND business growth, it would have lasting and impactful results. We can change the world. This is how women thrive in business. It's not by working from 7-7 everyday or wearing skirts to work (for goodness sake!). It's by creating our own futures and by working hard – whenever the heck we want! It's about making our own decisions and being of service to the world. And, for me, it's about fulfilling my life-long wish to be a mom.

I knew I wanted to be there when my kids got home from school. It's my choice. And, while, yes, there are times that I find myself hiding in the closet to make a business call, it's what I choose. It makes me happy. This is an important part of the fuel that runs my business.

My family is everything to me. In fact, I will never forget the last time I saw my Great Grandpa Julien. I have a decent-sized family and there were a lot of us there to visit him on one very special day. He was 100 years old. With his hair all disheveled, his shirt buttons mismatched, he stretched his arms out to his sides as if he was taking the whole world into his frail but hearty embrace. He said, "Look at this. Look at you all! I came to America from Belgium, just me and my wife, and look at what I built. Look at my family." It still brings me to tears. He did it! He built the life he wanted by taking bold leaps, and walking right over fear of the unknown.

I invite you to see what is possible. I've made it my mission to help women entrepreneurs everywhere reach their own true potential in business and in life.

I want you to feel the same balance and fulfillment. You deserve it!

Here's to Your Life•Business•Growth!

Kerry Swetmon is a Small Business Strategist with more than 15 years' experience serving entrepreneurs. As a graduate of The University of Florida, Kerry possesses a

Bachelor's Degree in Business Management, as well as Certifications in The Law of Attraction (Master) and Inbound Marketing. She has a passion for online systems and marketing and has devoted countless hours helping entrepreneurs grow their business to the million-dollar mark and beyond.
http://www.lifebusinessgrowth.com/

"Life is short and unpredictable, so embrace it. Shake the world up. Be the one to shock rather than be shocked."

- Ada Austin

In Memoriam: Ada Austin

This is a story about Ada Austin, who passed away in November of 2012. The moral of the story isn't to wait to do what you dream – instead be bold and jump in with both feet no matter what others (including family) may say.

To say the least, Ada was a challenging and exciting woman. Throughout her life she tried to make "no woman has held that job before" an antiquated phrase. Over the course of her life she held varied positions, such as Deputy Sherriff and Dispatcher, novice accordion player, waitress, bartender, ambulance (EMT) crew, semi-truck driver, pub & grill owner, wallpaper hanger, house painter, and office/home cleaner. She was a respite care provider, nursing assistant, and chauffer. She enjoyed breaking gender barriers in her jobs and didn't mind doing traditional work as well.

Ada enjoyed a tidy house and some say she left behind a honey-do list that could make the entire Armed Forces weep. She taught her children more than any boot camp training could on how to "square a place away." Ada had some powerful lungs she used for instruction, leaving her children un-phased by any drill instructors' "encouragement" throughout their army boot camp stints.

An animal lover, she had a myriad of family pets. Ada loved and raised Arabian show horses, Shar-Pei and Great Pyrenees dogs. She truly found her niche raising Angora goats, Babydoll sheep, Silky and Fainting Goats, and helped to breed the Navajo Churro Sheep back from near extinction. What these critters lacked in intellect they made up with genuine adoration and devotion to their caretaker.

As the owner of Austin's Mohair and Gifts, people all over knew who the "Old Goat Woman" in purple was, and where to buy her world-famous Mohair socks. And while LOCATION! LOCATION! LOCATION! is usually the chant, when she started this business, she didn't really think of that too much. She was ready to make the leap, and folks joined the team. Next thing you know, she had the King of Jordan standing under her willow tree with her husband feeding sheep and goats!

Ada found time to reach out to others in the trying times of their lives. She instinctively knew what people needed. Whether it was to give them a lift up, put them at ease, give them a job, make them know she felt that they mattered, or to just to "cuff 'em" – a classic Turnmire gesture - she'd do whatever it took to get them back up and moving on with their lives.

Near the end of her life, Ada had brain surgery for a glioblastoma tumor, a very aggressive cancer. When Ada twisted her doctor's arm for a guess of approximately how much time she'd get if she took treatments he replied, "a few months." She touched his hand and blustered "What the hell!" and looked to the family to support her decision not to take any treatments – as if she thought they would do anything else.

Ada and Jim celebrated 50 years together as husband and wife – a true team. Ada would say that this was their greatest accomplishment. When asked how she felt about it being her last year as the "Old Goat Woman" she would get teary-eyed and say, "It's been fun."

Ada left her body to science. Cancer has taken many of the people Ada loved, not just her own life, so she donated her body to the University of Minnesota. She sincerely hoped that their research would lead to a cure for glioblastoma and help the next generation of those inflicted.

Ada was disappointed that she was unable, due to health, to travel in the RV purchased to roam the country with Jim. Perhaps without meaning, she taught us not to put off 'til tomorrow what we should do today.

Lessons Ada enjoyed teaching were: "Family is everything, so stick together. Get an education because they can't take that away. Life is short and unpredictable, so embrace it. Shake the world up. Be the one to shock rather than be shocked."

Special thank you to Ada's daughters Tori and Konya who gave us permission and blessing to share this story.

Portions of this story previously published in The Fillmore County Journal.
http://fillmorecountyjournal.com/single.php?article_id=29038

"The difference between 'knowing' and 'doing' has been proclaiming it out loud, and claiming what I do and calling it mine."
- Connie Larson

Let Go and Live, Because...Now I am BIG!

By Connie Larson

My granddaughter, Brynnlee, recently turned four and so excited was she to be another year older. For weeks we heard her say in every situation, "Now I am big". When I reached down to hold her hand to cross the street, she pulled her hand from mine and looked up at me declaring, "I don't need to hold your hand, Nana, I am four and I am big!" She could do her own buckles on her car seat, she could ride a two-wheel bike (with training wheels), and she could sleep on the top bunk all because she **knew**,

"I am four and I am big!"

Not so long ago and yet almost a life time ago, I was suddenly single and free to follow whatever direction I wanted to go. I had a successful business in the corporate world of finance and yet I knew it was time to move on, to head in the direction of the yearnings of my heart. I didn't know what it was or even what it looked like until Easter 2007. I was sharing the day and a beautiful dinner with my single girlfriends and it just so happened that there among us was a career coach. At the end of the day, she looked at me and said, "Life Coach. That is what you are. It is a perfect fit for you".

My heart leapt in recognition with a resounding "YES!" That very night I found Martha Beck's Life Coach School and certification program. I knew of her, I had read her books, and I felt the connection. It was perfect until I discovered that the class was full. Heartbroken, I put my name on the waiting list and put it out of my mind.

The very next day, I received an email letting me know that there had been a cancelation and an open spot. Walking-on-sunshine happiness exploded in my soul until the PayPal link popped up. How would I pay for this? I would have to pay in full to hold my reservation and not once had I considered the cost. This is where the whisperings had lead, so believing it would happen, I relaxed into the calm reassurance that everything would be okay. Later that week, it was more than okay when I received a tax refund in the amount of my tuition.

School was great. I studied intensely and fell in love as my heart found its way home. My education was empowering and healing while I was making soul connections from every corner of the world. I loved being coached and learning how to live a better way, daring to open the door to my life while getting real and honest.

Two things happened at this point as my confidence took a back seat and I took a detour. The real estate market crashed and almost instantly my money was gone. Investments made were worthless and I had nothing left to fund my dream. At the same time one of my coaches asked me who my 'Ideal Client' was as part of my training to create my coaching business. I thought, "What better way to know her than to serve her?" I went to my favorite retail store and in two and a half years, I went from part-time Christmas help to store manager.

It paid the bills and I found my 'Ideal Client' but in the process I forgot ME.

At some point along the way, my back complained loudly about the pain caused from walking miles and miles in my own shoes. Heels and concrete were the source of my pain - or was it?

I pushed myself until I could push no longer. The pain was too great and my doctor sat me down to say, "You can get a new knee, you can even get a new hip, but you can never have a new back." I got it! I left my job to take care of my back.

All along I had coaching clients here and there, I was teaching classes online and I continued my own writing but I so was exhausted from working all day that I could barely put myself back together again on my days off. My son, the wise soul that he is, would ask me continuously when I would take my passion and my education seriously and do the work I was meant to do. I would look at him, and give him the head nod and quietly say, "I know, I know. Someday I will, Honey. Seriously, I will."

Now with my back at rest I faced new challenges. I was healing my body and at the same time we were now healing the soul of my son. He had asked, and we provided help, for his recovery from addiction. Perfect timing. It was there, while he was in a Christian-based treatment center, that we were able to visit every Sunday, a privilege that would not have been mine had I still been at work.

Before I left after each visit, Austin would pray for me that I would be safe traveling home, that my back would be healed and that I would finally use my education and talent in helping others. He prayed that I find a way to walk in the path of my passion of helping women step into their own power. I just had to step into my very own.

This son of mine, a very wise soul, loaned to me for just a short time, has now moved on to his next life, his next chapter, so how could I not step into mine? I stepped up my pace, claimed my place in this world, had already left my job and was ready to step into my right life.

I left my retail and corporate jobs behind to listen to my heart and follow my purpose. The difference between 'knowing' and 'doing' has been proclaiming it out loud, and claiming what I do and calling it mine. No more did I need to have one foot in each door, relying on my job as my safety net. One door had to shut for the other to fully open. Just like a firefly, when we are trapped, our light goes out. It is upon our release that not only do we fly, but we light the way.

I took the time to create my business full-time. I took the time to say I am available for workshops, to teach in the community, to write and be published, to work on the books that have only been ideas in my head, and to literally help other women step back into their own power.

My formula:

See it

Feel it

Trust it

Do it

BE it.

If my four year grandbaby could do anything just because she believed it so with no limits and no doubting, I could follow her lead. I let go and said, "I can because I am 52 and I am BIG."

"And when she finally said NO enough times, she let go and said YES!"

My work is dedicated to my children who light the way.

Connie Larson is a certified life coach, speaker and author specializing in empowering individuals' transition through life's challenges.

She currently lives in sunny southern California with her partner, the love of her life, where they the share the joy of nine children, 12 grandchildren, one dog, and one cat. She considers herself blessed and privileged to spend her time following her passion, hanging out with amazing people, and living her dreams. Connect with Connie at connie.larson2@facebook.com

There was always lots of dancing. We shared a freedom of expression that is innately joyous in all of us.

- Mary Sommerset

Letting Go and Embracing the "Now"

By Mary Sommerset

Finding my passion came after working in corporations and small businesses. Although I enjoyed my work in developing strategic partnerships and analyzing research for a global software company, I wanted to give something back. Maybe it was my Irish Catholic upbringing or maybe it was watching the news and seeing so many women in the world without basic freedoms I took for granted. In any case, I was inspired to become a business coach.

The training and certification process for coaching was a great "half-way house" to achieve my goal. Coaching is very fulfilling in that it is possible to assist others to tap into their own understanding of who they are and who they want to become. I was maintaining my coaching career, yet once again, that was not enough. I wanted to reach more people - specifically, more women.

I was looking online for women's groups, thinking I could expand my coaching business in that direction. I found BraveHeart Women and began watching the television shows with the founder, Ellie Drake, and various celebrities and successful business people. Webinars were also available on the site. I thought to myself, "Well, if I learn something new, I'll be interested." Not that I was jaded; however, so much of the same information on personal growth seems to circulate on the web.

For the first time, I heard about oxytocin, a natural hormone in our bodies, often considered the loving/bonding hormone, which Ellie and team were teaching women how to release intentionally. That was new for me; I was intrigued.

The next webinar I listened to introduced me to BraveHeart Women's international conference in Los Angeles held each November. Ellie said, "If you really want to know what's going on with BraveHeart Women, then come to this conference and find out." I tapped into my intuition and went.

I bought an Early Bird ticket at a great price and hopped on a plane from Portland to Los Angeles. I walked in the conference the first night and met Ellie with a soul-to-soul connection through the eyes. I thoroughly enjoyed myself and made connections with women from all different backgrounds. I was opened up to a whole new experience.

At the time, I had been keeping an eye out for a retreat, one that would offer some transformational elements as I was entering a new phase of life.

I went to this retreat not knowing all the details yet knowing in my bones that I was committed to releasing old patterns, images, conversations, and more that I had stored in my body. I also wanted to stop crying so easily. I really didn't know why I was "crying on a nickel" as some friends' teased. I did intend to stop it, however.

The leaders were very skilled at leading us through exercises and experiences unique to this process. I let go of so much unnecessary suffering that when I returned home I immediately lost 10 pounds and improved my relationships. My husband likes to joke that "the body-snatchers" got me.

In the past, I had worked on several global projects, yet each time I got burnt out. I needed joy in my life to thrive. There was no denying the joy I experienced with my BraveHeart sisters on this retreat. There was always lots of dancing. We shared a freedom of expression that is innately joyous in all of us.

I created my own online community to assist others in seeing obstacles in a new way and embracing the present while letting go of the past. It helped myself as well. It is a great way to share your knowledge, connect with women globally, and build your brand.

Inspiration from my hundreds of members led to my writing a book, *Letting Go For Fun & Profit: How Advances in Neuroscience Inspire Change.* The pictures of the mind now prove that we can change our neural pathways for the better with consistent action. The research fascinated me. I asked my sister, who has 25 years in the public health industry, to co-write the book with me. Jean has witnessed many changes in the people she has worked with – even developing programs for whole cities!

Ellie asked me to be on stage at the BraveHeart Women conference in 2012 and I was able to tell this story of moving from not knowing what I was going to do next to experiencing a transformational retreat, attending another training on a cruise ship to the Caribbean, creating an online community, and writing a book.

All this because I said, "Yes!"

+Thus, beginning with coaching and then moving forward with BraveHeart Women, my brand as a Change Agent was created.

Last year BraveHeart Women decided to pioneer local chapters for women to meet in person. Ellie asked me to be a local leader in my home city, Portland, Oregon. Again, I said, "Yes!"

The nine day training was a deep dive into both the personal growth required for the role and the business of creating a chapter from the ground up. The curriculum for the courses offered each month would come from the BraveHeart Women office. Our group was the first one to go through this training. In a very real sense, we were pioneering this effort. Our Portland Chapter is ten months old and growing.

In May of 2014, I will travel to Israel to participate in a project involving 1000 women participating in Oxytocin Circles For Peace. The participants will be equal numbers of Western women, Israeli women, and Palestinian women. The event will even be filmed as part of a documentary.

When I look back on this process, it brings a smile to my face. I am filled with gratitude for finding my passion. I know in my heart that when women rise, we all rise. Our time is now.

Mary Sommerset promotes positive change with significant results as she works with business owners, entrepreneurs, executives, managers, employees and more. Employing an engaging interactive approach, Mary motivates individuals and organizations to take on fresh perspectives; to shift the way they see, hear and think about the work they do.
https://clearstreamcoaching.com/

"Being courageous is not easy but the rewards are great. Since giving up my job I have experienced a different kind of stress but the excitement and rewards that come from making decisions from my heart instead of my head have been so worth it."

- Carol LeBlanc

Flexing My Courage Muscle

By Carol LeBlanc

I have always been a good girl and played things safe. I've always worked hard and tried to be nice and sweet and pleasing just like my momma taught me. Then I grew up and found this just doesn't work. It's dishonest and constantly denies who you really are. If you don't speak your mind or share your opinions because of the fear of being disliked then you are denying your true self. Once I realized this, I felt so unsettled. I knew that the way I had been operating for my entire life had to change.

I could not remain the same now that I had this knowledge. I had to learn to express myself even though it scared the hell out of me. I started forcing myself to say things like, "I disagree" and "That won't work for me". The more I did this, the easier it got. I got stronger and more confident. I began to discover who I really was and what I believed in. I started having more authentic interactions and deeper relationships. For the first time in my life, I encountered people who didn't like me. I forced myself to have the courage to not have pleasing others be my highest goal. I began to show my true self.

I've always wanted to be an entrepreneur. I watched my father run his own business and am strongly attracted to the energy of entrepreneurs. They are so alive and are constantly creating. The fearless energy of the entrepreneur is so different from who I was and who I was taught to be. I wanted this. I wanted to create. I wanted to stand for something. I could feel that the person I was meant to be was locked inside me, crying out to be born, dying to be expressed. I took a college assessment that told me that I was 98% suited to be an entrepreneur.

Entrepreneurship ranked far and above any other thing I could do with my life but still I continued on the safe path until I was shown that it was no longer safe.

I worked for a tax and audit firm for four years and was told two weeks after tax season that my job was being reduced because of the lack of cash flow. This rocked my world and was the beginning of the end of my life as an employee. I started listening to inspirational recordings through headphones at my desk to fill myself with the belief that I could do this while blocking out the negative energy of my workplace. I brainwashed myself into believing in my skills and gifts. I began to believe that it was possible for me to create something that no one person could take away with two days' notice. I had something to offer the world that was bigger and more impactful than what I could deliver in exchange for a paycheck. My belief was growing but now I needed the courage to quit.

I started to strengthen my courage muscle. I listened to motivational speakers like Ali Brown and David Neagle talk about the Laws of the Universe and leaps of faith. "Jump and the bridge will appear" and all that jazz. I started taking action and putting myself on the spot. I began investing in myself and expecting a return on that investment. I started believing that I could help people and that I had a duty to live my life as directed by God rather than by fear. I was trying to muster up the courage to give up the false sense of safety that my job offered.

Being courageous is not easy but the rewards are great. Since giving up my job I have experienced a different kind of stress but the excitement and rewards that come from making decisions from my heart instead of my head have been so worth it. I had the courage to quit. I had the courage to go backwards in order to go forward. I had the courage to act as my spirit directed when I could not see the details of how things would work out. It's like driving down a foggy road. I know it's the right road but I can only see the next few feet.

I don't know the end of the story yet but I do know that it feels right. I do know that I am free to provide greater value to my customers than I was allowed to as an employee. Now I have time to create something new and useful that is truly helpful and improves the lives of others. As an entrepreneur, I am constantly presented with new situations where I get to exercise my courage muscle. I continue to do the hard work that I am afraid to do, and every time I tell my fear to take a hike and do something difficult, I am rewarded with a richness of experience that was missing from my safe people-pleasing life. Now the words coming out of my mouth might be hard for me to say and hard for others to hear but they are honest and spoken in the spirit of service with the highest good for everyone in my heart.

Based in Albany, New York, Carol LeBlanc is passionate about supporting entrepreneurs with their accounting as an integral part of their business team. She offers virtual bookkeeping services, QuickBooks training, strategic planning and coaching for women entrepreneurs around pricing and value. Carol specializes in caring about the people she works with and getting them accurate financial information.
www.carolleblanccpa.com

"When you have the right attitude, NEVER give up on your dreams, and truly LOVE your own life, the most caring, beautiful people, situations, and even creative inspiration and an abundance of miracles all start showing up more than you can ever imagine!"
- Tara Ursulescu

It's All About Passion!

By Tara Ursulescu

"Passion is energy. Feel the power that comes from focusing on what excites you." - *Oprah Winfrey*

Ahh passion! I truly do not know another topic I am more passionate about than passion! Passion is soo exciting! To ourselves when we feel it, but also to those around us witnessing our excitement! It excites, ignites, fires up, and lights up our very soul! Life is beautiful, more colorful and brighter when we have passion. To me, passion is Life! It is a growing, living, breathing entity in itself - much like a relationship. It may start with a thought or a spark of inspiration, but there is something so magical and miraculous that occurs when we've been touched by passion - like God, the angels, or the Universe itself are smiling upon us, sending us positive vibes and blessings! Passion is ENERGY. It is powerful. Like any form of power, we need to be aware of how we are focusing our passion - will it be for the greater good of yourself, your life, and others? If so, you will be blessed and fully provided for along your fantastic adventure! Love is the goal, and passion is the energy behind it to drive us towards it even on days we don't feel so motivated.

My journey of following my passion in life has been an ongoing internal battle. Though I tried to do the "right" thing and follow the standards we accept from society, our family, friends, even our partners, I knew deep in my heart that I needed to live a more passionate life than the traditional 9 to 5 career that was expected of me. I ignored that small but persistent voice, swatting it away like an annoying fly. I was being "trained" in university to change my views and the way I thought and looked at the world – to be more logical and scientific. I didn't quite understand at the time how that would fit into my dream of wanting to help others as a counselor or psychologist – didn't that mean I should be more intuitive and listen to my heart? I didn't get it, and the five years I was in university were tough on me in many ways. Thankfully, near the end of my schooling, classes started getting a lot more interesting for me as I started speaking up and writing about my interest in the spiritual world, and developing my skills in intuition.

I spent an extra year in school, conducting research on Highly Sensitive People, and how that character trait can affect their self-esteem – thankfully, a topic I am very passionate about. I was fortunate to have two extremely unique and special psychology professors who taught the higher levels of psychology classes in a very unorthodox fashion. We sat in healing circles, not desks, passed around a feather or a rock when it was our time to speak, learning to honor every single person's contribution and heart-felt thoughts and stories. We were taught how valuable it was to be sensitive and empathic, and how to develop active listening skills to not only better serve clients, but also our friends and loved ones as well.

I wanted to be a counselor who used humanistic and client-centered therapies which empowered clients to make their own decisions and put them in full charge of their own lives, to help them get in touch with their own inner knowing, not tell them what I thought they should do or think. I didn't want to practice from the viewpoint of portraying that I had the answers to their problems, and that they needed to listen to me in order to get well. I learned that by providing a safe space and unconditional positive regard for them, clients would open up and realize their own answers by following their intuition, using me only as their guide. My passion for helping people at a deep soul level was ignited!

There was so much more I wanted to learn when it came to truly helping others live lives they were deeply passionate about! I had, and still have, such a deep thirst and curiosity for learning as much as I can when it comes to inspiring others, and being inspired by others as well, and to be my best self and make a change in the world somehow. I knew I wanted to help empower women and help us all learn how to fully step into our beautiful selves as the loving, caring, kind, and powerful women we can be!

By some miracle, when I finally graduated, I managed to be mostly an A-student throughout school, even winning a university prize for Most Distinguished Student in the Faculty of Arts. The only thing was, I won it, kicking and screaming! As a perfectionist and over-achiever, I was constantly stressed out, and on the road to complete burn-out. The education was so worth it however, and I'd do it all over again, though perhaps with a more kind, accepting, self-loving, calmer, healthier attitude towards myself.

Soon after graduation, I started a Master's degree in Counseling, but again, I felt I really wanted to *get out there* in life, meet people, and really *talk* to them – and not about the topics I found superficial and shallow. I wanted to know how they were *really* doing, what kinds of challenges had they overcome – and how did they do it? So many questions I had! I jumped at the chance to utilize my qualitative interviewing skills, humanistic and client-centered education, active listening skills, and huge desire to interview others on overcoming their challenges when I was offered a job as a Field Director with a film company. My job was to interview survivors of natural disasters (e.g.; plane crashes, shipwrecks, volcanic eruptions) for a television documentary called *Disasters of the Century*. The interviews were later shown on The Discovery Channel.

I was able to travel around Eastern Canada and the United States, and I thought it was my dream job! My assignments ended up not being consistent enough for me to make a living, but I greatly enjoyed my experience. I also worked for a journalist for four years, lining up interviews and writing for various newspapers and small magazines. I loved it! The money wasn't great but I sure loved the independence, working all hours of the night if I wanted, and mostly – meeting interesting people, from small business owners to professional athletes to the premier of Saskatchewan. Back then, however, I thought that in order to help people, meant I needed to work incredible amounts of overtime (often unpaid), and put 110% of my energy – my Life - ME! – into work.

Thinking success meant I needed to make more money and get into the corporate world, I eventually went on to work for various government agencies in areas of social work, human resources, and later on, as Recruitment Consultant. Eventually, I was hiring hundreds of employees and became a coach/consultant for fifty-plus school principals, and to dozens of managers at a hospital. Over-giving, working overtime, and constantly learning new roles as a contractor took its toll. I got burnt out in every way possible – emotionally, physically, and spiritually. I was exhausted!

It should not have come as a surprise however; I was working up to seventy hours a week, and while I was being paid the most money I had ever earned, I was still only getting paid for thirty-five hours a week. That's how crazy I was! The workload was not only incredibly unrealistic, but people were leaving in handfuls so we were in a staff-shortage crisis. Of course, I thought I could pick up the slack, even without being given an assistant like I had been advised upon accepting the contract. I remember with clear distinction, receiving over 1100 emails per month, all with demands for my help. The clients I were helping, and the organization I was currently with, were all in crisis, and would often share their extreme frustration, tears, and anger at the office politics of which I had no part, being a temporary contractor. I began dreading picking up the phone or turning my computer on.

Living off of caffeine, espressos, skipping lunch, living indoors in front of my computer and phone, with very little fresh air and sunlight, I started developing vitamin deficiencies, chronic insomnia, and anxiety. Work was becoming a serious threat to my health. I also was becoming more and more miserable even though I had doubled my income in one year. My relationship suffered, and my health was starting to deteriorate. I was constantly tired and exhausted, though I continued to push myself harder and harder at work. It felt like I kept attracting very difficult or challenging positions, and people in the workplace. It seemed all of the organizations were in crisis! Many of my friends would say they had no idea how I could handle some of the assignments or contracts I had. Eventually, I started getting anxious going to work and felt like a huge part of my heart and soul was missing.

Thankfully I started seeing a naturopathic doctor five years ago and am still taking supplements and following a specific diet for adrenal exhaustion, which also affected my thyroid, not to mention soul-burn out. One naturopath told me that, internally, I was run down and that my organs were over 60 years old – and I was only in my 30s! NOT GOOD! I certainly felt it.

Another nutritionist told me I would literally ***die*** if I didn't change my eating habits and start taking better care of myself! I had been following a certain way of eating (which I fully believed to be healthy) but was told that due to my certain body chemistry, it was NOT the right fit for me. My body was damaging itself internally as it was looking for the right nutrients! Blood tests were coming back with poor results, showing my body was getting more and more run down with chronic stress that I had not learned how to cope with.

It was time – beyond time – for me to take a good hard look at my life choices and career.

When my contract ran out, the organization I worked for was shocked that I didn't want to renew it again! I didn't know how I was going to do it, but I was determined to find work that I loved deep within my Soul. I started sending my writing portfolio to a couple magazines. Like a dream come true, I found one that was EXACTLY what I was looking for and was told they'd be printing one of my articles right away! Instead of writing one article per monthly issue like most writers, of course I overdid it at first, and would submit two or three! I am still learning to go slowly, relax into the process, and most importantly - how to take care of myself, my body, health, mind, body, and Soul. I am focusing more on being and feeling peaceful rather than the crazy rat race of the corporate world and downtown traffic that gets my adrenalin pumping but not always in a way that's good for me. My highly sensitive body does not thrive well in loud crowded environments, nor do I function at my best when I am working at a job that doesn't feed my Soul.

Now, miracles upon miracles keep happening and I have been able to heal in many ways since I took time off for myself to listen to my heart.

Today, I am so much more relaxed and happy you might not recognize me! I work from home as a freelance writer and editor, and am the Editor-in-Chief of SoulWoman eMagazine, spiritual inspiration for women (and men!) around the world, which is a dream job for me!! I also reached another goal of mine last year and got my Certified Coach Practitioner certificate. I LOVE what I do, am far more healthier and relaxed, and I take time every day to get outside in Nature and give such thanks every single day for the blessings I have in my life. I have so many more dreams that I will follow, including writing my own book. I am currently co-editing THIS book as well, and I couldn't be more thrilled or honored to be in such amazing company as these beautiful courageous women! I also have another two books to review this month and possibly edit or even write in the near future for amazing people across the globe, on topics that fire me up just thinking about it!

If you are not on the right path for your Soul, you WILL feel chronically exhausted!

Giving your time, energy and PASSION to doing what you LOVE, is the best gift you can give yourself! You will feel more ENERGY, HAPPINESS, & JOY! My life is not perfect by any means, but right now – it is truly a blessing and gift that I am grateful for every day! When you have the right attitude, NEVER give up on your dreams, and truly LOVE your own life, the most caring, beautiful people, situations, and even creative inspiration and an abundance of miracles all start showing up more than you can ever imagine! Thank you to all of YOU who have journeyed with me and who have encouraged me to keep following my passion!

It is my heart's desire and deep passion to help inspire and empower women and men around the world in a way that is loving, caring, soulful, and real.

Tara Ursulescu, an empath, is a passionate & inspirational writer - with an edge! She holds a Bachelor's Degree (Honors) in Psychology, and is a Certified Coach Practitioner. She currently resides in Calgary, Canada.

One of her many passions includes meeting and interviewing inspirational people and sharing their stories through her writing. Visit her at her new website at http://taralifewriter.wordpress.com where you will find many of her published articles from Soulwoman eMagazine, and more.

https://www.facebook.com/pages/Inspirational-Life-Writer-Tara-Ursulescu/328450753943100

Part 4: Life By Your Own Design

Do you like to take charge versus letting others do the planning for you? Do you follow a different beat than the rest of the crowd? Do you desire to live your life your own way and to earn a living by following your own passion?

Entrepreneurs often have strong convictions and motivations. They won't let others tell them that something can't be done. They don't want to play office politics or wait for managerial approval. They want to work on their own terms free from the stresses of corporate life.

Many entrepreneurs leave the traditional workforce so they can live authentically and be true to themselves. They don't fit the conventional pattern, nor do they want to. These business owners want to live life in their own unique way and on their own personal schedule.

They have a vision of what life should look like. Perhaps it involves the freedom to travel and work from any place in the world. Maybe it's the flexibility to spend time with friends and family. For whatever their personal reason, they follow their hearts regardless of societal and cultural expectations.

The stories in this final section all feature women who decided to take the leap into small business ownership so they could live unconventionally and do what they wanted to do. They decided to pursue a life without regrets and painful thoughts about what "might have been." They wanted to live a life of their own design.

Picture your ideal life. What would you do if you knew nothing could hold you back? Once you have it visualized, determine the true steps to getting there, separated out from the fears and emotional barriers that are in your head. Avoid getting overwhelmed by the scariness of the big picture by breaking these steps down into small individual pieces and work on accomplishing each task one at a time. By celebrating small achievements on the way to your overall goal, you can move past your fears and begin the work of achieving your dreams.

You only live once. Make it count. Live a life of your own design and live a life unbound!

"Even though being an entrepreneur is in no way the easiest path, it is a very true path. There is nowhere to hide—and that's a good thing."

- Madeleine Eno

On Letting Yourself Be Seen

By Madeleine Eno

I came of age, professionally speaking, in the era of teal shoulder pad blazers and crisp resumes printed on thick, cream-colored paper.

In those days, my friends and I walked in sneakers and nylons to the subway—taking the Green or Red Line into Boston, changing into pumps in neat cubicles. The boss treated us to the occasional steak and martini lunch and quitting time was firmly 5 p.m.

Authenticity wasn't a blip on the radar. As for being vulnerable, being seen and standing out... it was more like "never let 'em see you sweat."

These were days of doing the things that others had done before in order to get a predictable and pleasing result. My cubicle mate, Ann, for instance, who chain-smoked as she tapped away at her Electric typewriter, had quickly spun up the corporate ladder and would give me advice on how to do it right, namely who to schmooze.

But despite the path to workplace predictability and stability that she and others laid out so temptingly before me, I gravitated toward the big, maverick ideas. I pitched the outside-the-box proposals.

This may sound cool. Trust me, in that setting, it really wasn't. I was way better at generating big ideas than following through on them. After Ann packed up her lunch things and went home on time, I burned a lot of lonely midnight and weekend oil in our cubicle.

But while my 9 to 5 habits were already looking entrepreneurial, and while I did all kinds of side jobs (wedding invitation calligrapher, English teacher, chiropractic receptionist, waitress, house cleaner), I don't remember ever thinking of starting my own business.

Outside of cafes and record stores, I didn't even *know* people who had businesses.

And more than that, I didn't get that I had the *power* to run my own business. I think that is why I had all those schemes and part-time jobs... If I diffused myself and spread myself *very* thin, I never had to succeed at any of them. I never had to be seen.

It's what I now call the "scramble" technique of living. We spend our time scrambling to handle the emergencies, deadlines, and dramas that are in front of us and never catch a breath or a glimpse of the big picture. Running from what's meaningful, we never get to know our real purpose in the world.

But as they say, you can run but you cannot hide...

I eventually took a job with a small design firm owned by two cool women and started learning what it took to run a small business. But they were stressed because it had become something that didn't allow them much freedom. A big printing company bought them out, office politics reigned supreme, and any entrepreneurial sizzle fizzled.

A few years later, I found a wonderful job as the editor of an outdoor magazine. This would have been a perfect, creative, and adventurous job in which to grow old. I loved it and worked with an amazing team.

Part of me could have stayed there forever. But another part of me attended a nature writers' retreat in the Sierras, which led me to fall in love with a mountain poet, which led me to sell everything, follow my heart and move to rural Oregon.

My boss encouraged me to keep my job, so I telecommuted from a tiny cabin on Mount Hood to downtown Boston, via a whistling, clanking dial-up modem. I could actually take a decent hike on trails behind my house while I was downloading page proofs.

Enter stage left: a couple of major heartbreaks and a lay-off... and I started cobbling together the part-time jobs again—now teaching art, teaching yoga and bartending.

It was fun, in an adrenaline-soaked, super-scrambled way. And it kept me very small. Hidden. It's hard to be big or noticed when you have to run to another gig in 15 minutes.

I raced from job to volunteer post to classroom. I couldn't seem to stop of my own accord. So I did what any non-self-respecting, overscheduled and overwhelmed potential entrepreneur would do...

I got sick.

So sick, in fact, that I had to quit most of what I was doing. And I ended up with a large chunk of time in which to think. When I couldn't run anymore, I could finally look at what I was running from.

Lying in my bed, I had a flash. I realized that no matter what else I was doing, almost throughout my whole life, I was writing for other people—scribbling business plans, crafting mission statements, jotting down taglines.

There was that thread through all of it. It was like a thread of sanity, of meaning—even when I was in the midst of the greatest scramble times.

And I also saw that being of service had always been vital to me... I tried to be the most responsive bartender, the yoga teacher who came around and gave foot massages during sivasana, the art instructor who brought awesome snacks.

When I put it together, I saw that I could be of service through my writing. That my writing could be a service to the world.

Whoa. That's what I'd been running from.

I saw that this thread could be my *golden* thread.

I let myself think, "what if..." I hung out my shingle as a writer for business-owners. I let myself be seen. I made the leap.

Picture my leap in slow-mo... something that took about 15 years. Or maybe it was more like being lowered gingerly off a cliff, and bouncing hard against the rocky side until I landed at the bottom.

Regardless, the truth of what I was designed to do gently knocked and waited, knocked a little harder, then harder still—waiting for me to come around.

I recently launched a program called the Golden Thread. I believe finding that thread in our story can be the source of enormous meaning and power in our lives.

I love this Adyashanti quote: "Truth replaces you. It takes up residence." For me, that's how it's been. I have been replaced, bit by bit, by the truth of being an entrepreneur. By living my purpose and serving the world by helping others tell *their* truth.

As that truth took up residence in me, I gradually stopped looking at part-time jobs on craigslist. I started meeting incredible people who helped me (and hired me.) The dramas around me miraculously subsided. I began making money. I felt myself relaxing into being me. A me who was free and alive and self-determined.

My belief isn't that everyone needs to be or should be an entrepreneur.

But I do believe that if you're meant to be one, your way will be shown, your own path will appear, as will the helpers to lead the way.

Even though being an entrepreneur is in no way the easiest path, it is a very true path. There is *nowhere* to hide—and that's a good thing.

And every single day that truth takes up a little more of you.

Madeleine Eno is a writing and marketing strategist from Portland, Oregon who helps brilliant but unseen business owners define your message, develop an action plan, and get written projects like these into the world, so your ideal clients can find you. Please visit her at www.inthewriteplace.com

"In fact, the lessons I learned performing have helped me become successful in life. For one thing, being a clown taught me the importance of believing in my own story."

- Leslie Ann Akin

A Life of Art, Music, and Smiles

By Leslie Ann Akin

Primarily, my journey has been an aesthetic one but informed with an entertainer's sensibilities. I love and appreciate all forms of art – music, drama, and fine art – and I've lived a life devoted to that vision. In the early seventies, I was a mother with two kids living in the suburbs but I never let that define me. I was a mother with two kids, yes, but I was also a professional clown. That's right, I was a circus arts performer, dodging swinging mops and buckets of confetti, and yes, even pies.

I did comedy magic shows, juggling, instructed at clown conferences, and toured with a circus. I never let one take away from another. I loved my kids and was a good mother, but I was also a great clown. Actually, if you think about it, clowning and parenthood are two parts of a whole. Today my children are wonderful and successful adults and I got to spend my life making people laugh.

For six years I wrote for a national publication, Laugh Makers Magazine. My columns were about clown character development, the funny business of being funny, skits, magic, costumes, props, and lessons I had learned while performing. And believe me, I learned a lot.

People may think that being a clown is a trivial occupation but quite the opposite is true. In fact, the lessons I learned performing have helped me become successful in life. For one thing, being a clown taught me the importance of believing in my own story.

With my clown persona, I had license to playfully remind people of their humanity. Taking pies in the face and running around the hippodrome track as if my pants were on fire was business as usual. Once I removed the makeup, I was the charming housewife I was expected to be. This kind of role switching requires a huge amount of awareness and self-discipline. In addition, I learned to read an audience. I developed a keen sense of my audience's energy and how to play off their vibe.

Finally, my juggling, plate spinning, and comedy magic show, complete with Domino the Dynamic Wonder Bunny, taught me that timing is everything. To pull off these shows, I had to be prepared to respond to whatever happened within a split second. Awareness, self-discipline, understanding one's audience, going with the moment: all these lessons have been invaluable in my life.

During the Carter and Reagan administrations, I was invited to perform at The White House and bring my team of pranksters - a genuine honor. I'll always remember the puzzled look on the secret service man's face as he sorted through my wacky, over-sized props, fire-orange wigs, and colossal shoes.

I also enjoyed performing at hospitals. In my role as Docktor FunnyBone, I made my rounds and performed for kids and adults alike. Sometimes I was animated, sometimes low-key, but I was always sure to be sensitive to the needs of my audience, and I never left before I'd brought a smile to the palest face. Those smiles are still with me today and remain one of the highlights of my life. I'm proud to have walked in the shoes of a clown for fourteen years.

My love of clowning began to give way to a passion for music, and when a juggler friend who hosted a show on a community radio station said I'd be a perfect candidate for a DJ because of my love and knowledge of jazz, I jumped at the chance. Sharing the music I loved was a real joy: Ella Fitzgerald, Count Basie, Dinah Washington, and Joe Williams – Wow!

I hosted my own four-hour radio program once a week. At noon I aired classic jazz jams that I dubbed "The Peanut Butter and Jam Session." It was so successful that I soon I landed an on-air position with a commercial jazz radio station where I produced programs in every time slot imaginable. My listeners encouraged me to go for the larger jazz radio station, so I did and landed a job as on-air talent and producer for a significant radio station. I fondly recall those twelve years of producing jazz and blues radio programs where I was lucky enough to interview many jazz legends.

As I learned in clowning, timing is everything, so when my husband Ron wanted to move back to his home in Oregon, I sensed he was right. It was time to leave the San Francisco Bay Area and move on from music to another passion of mine: graphic design. Graphics are the perfect marriage of fine arts and entertainment. To be a successful graphic artist you have to know your audience. And boy howdy had I learned how to do that!

In San Francisco, I had often created CD inserts for my deejay and music friends. Because of my experience in radio, and my understanding of graphics, I realized that CDs could yield more radio play if they were designed with a specific format. My articles were published in music trade magazines and were well received.

During the years that I clowned around and hosted a radio show, I had created my own marketing and print campaigns. Of course, this was back in the dark ages of light tables and paste-up but nevertheless, the basic design principals remain the same. My grasp of design and my ability to understand what my client wants, even if he or she can't verbalize it is something that comes naturally to me.

Ron and I owned a graphic design studio in Sutherlin, Oregon where we were so successful we were voted Business of the Year for 2007-2008. When we relocated to Lake Oswego, Oregon, in 2009, we became the little studio with the big vision and we've never looked back. Our mission is to change the world, one business card at a time. We have done that with a vengeance, helping our clients enlarge their business at the same time they enlarge their sense of self and their own capabilities. It's truly a joy to watch the transformations.

My designs help clients meet a variety of marketing needs. I request my clients' ideas, but I also request their trust. As I mentioned before, I have absolute faith in my artistic vision and it has never proved me wrong on my life's journey.

The Portland, Oregon area has proven to be the best location for my husband and myself, although I work with clients from other states as well. One of the best things to happen since being here is that through networking I met a woman named Jewels Muller. At that time she was a professional organizer and a brilliant force of nature when it came to networking. We chatted about how we felt after typical networking—like it had no soul. We wanted something with more depth, more meaning, not just a sale.

So Jewels created a mastermind group named Chicks Connect that brings women together in small groups to network and nurture each other. I love watching women pay attention to their whole beings, including personal growth and paying it forward. As we help each other, we help ourselves. I was honored when Jewels asked me to design their logo.

Chicks Connect focuses on personal growth, and has inspired me to be more authentic and willing to work on myself under the guidance of the curriculum and interactions with other members. Of course I have fun, but along the way I have made lasting friendships and learned how to be self-actualized. I leave meetings feeling more energized and more alive.

My other passion is practicing gratitude daily, personally and in business. It's made a huge difference in my life in every way possible by sending a real heartfelt greeting card to people I'm thinking about. These are people I want to celebrate and honor for their successes, and clients I want to thank for their business and referrals. Giving to give, not to get, has opened me up to greater possibilities.

I feel so lucky to be living my passion here in beautiful village of Lake Oswego, Oregon. I love making a difference; I love creating designs for businesses, and I love that I can make a living doing both. And if I haven't made you laugh by the end of our conversation, I have not done it correctly.

Leslie Ann Akin is the owner of Lake Oswego Graphics, the "little studio with big vision." Based out of Lake Oswego, Oregon, she works with clients in almost every state in the US as well as in Canada designing everything from business cards to billboards. Please visit her at: www.LakeOswegoGraphics.com

"Part of me felt that old pull to do this work full time, but the pay was about one-third of what I was currently making with the marketing firm, so I didn't even consider it. Yet, again, the Universe had other plans for me."

- Lisa Smith

Coaching of the Mind: My Path as a Hypnotist

By Lisa Smith

In 1989, I graduated from college with a Bachelor's degree in Marketing & Communications and a minor in Psychology. I soon got a job in the marketing department of a well-known local health insurance company outside of Boston. I worked there for two years before moving on to the marketing and editorial department of a large international market research firm in Boston. I worked there for seven years during which time I was promoted to head of the department. I loved the work and was very good at it, but my heart was being called in another direction.

Since high school I had an interest in the mind, self-improvement, and spirituality, and I read voraciously on these topics. I learned self-hypnosis and used it with myself first for fun then for a variety of ways to improve myself. Through college, I attended workshops and classes on meditation, hypnosis, channeling, and other alternative types of studies. While still working for the market research firm, I earned my certification as a hypnotherapist and began practicing on friends and family. Once they started to refer to me, I began to work with people I didn't know and to charge for it. Soon I secretly wondered what it would be like to do this full time, but I was too afraid to leave the "security" of a paycheck and try to open my own practice.

In 1997, I was getting strong feelings and unmistakable (even unbelievable) signs that I should move to Virginia Beach, where my dad and an organization I belonged to since college, the Association for Research and Enlightenment, both resided.

Despite fears of the unknown, leaving all my good friends and family, and all I had known for 20 years, I trusted the signs and that they were divinely guided to move me on the path to something different.

I had arranged with my employer to continue to work for them from Virginia, which gave me my first taste of telecommuting. I enjoyed the independence and freedom of working from home. I had always been a disciplined and dedicated worker, so I didn't have a problem creating a routine of getting my work done, even though I was at home.

Since I had my own place with two bedrooms, I turned one into an office and started to see hypnosis clients on occasion. The owner of a local hypnosis center told me at a hypnosis convention we were at that if I ever wanted a job to give him a call. Part of me felt that old pull to do this work full time, but the pay was about one-third of what I was currently making with the marketing firm, so I didn't even consider it. Yet, again, the Universe had other plans for me.

When some situations with the company created less and less work for me, I "saw the writing on the wall" and realized it was just a matter of time before I would be phased out. After being out of the 9 to 5 office job environment for almost a year, I really didn't want to lose that freedom and flexibility, and the lure of finally doing hypnosis full time was enough to make me willing to tighten my belt for a while to accept the job offer at the hypnosis clinic. Thankfully, they provided me with health insurance and I got a 50-cent raise every 6 months as long as I was doing well. That took away some of the sting of the huge pay cut as well as the feeling of finally being of service to people in a more meaningful way on a full-time basis. I was finally a full-time hypnotherapist!

I loved the company and its owners, the clients, the learning, the experience, the flexible schedule, and the way I grew during my time there. I was seeing an average of five clients a day and sometimes as many as eight. I started teaching their classes on self-hypnosis, psycholinguistics, and nutrition (for the weight loss clients) and working on my Master's in holistic nutrition. I also quit smoking and lost about 25 lbs. as a result of being in that environment and exposed to hypnotic suggestion nearly every day.

I started a company newsletter that was distributed to their franchise centers across the country and became one of their lead hypnotists. I earned my Master Hypnotherapist and Psycholinguistics Practitioner certifications, became trained and certified as a life coach, and started learning Emotional Freedom Technique (EFT).

It was an amazing time, though some management changes that occurred after several years made my time there more challenging, and I felt that urging to make a change and do this work for myself. Again, the fear of not being able to make a real business of it, get clients &

support myself was too strong to allow me to leave. But again, the Universe had bigger plans for me.

In 2006, two weeks before my 40th birthday, after nearly eight years at the hypnosis center, I learned that they were closing the two centers in Virginia (which had been taken over by someone else two years earlier) and I found myself at a crossroads – either try to get a job back in the corporate world in my former field of marketing, or finally strike out on my own as a self-employed hypnotherapist and coach.

I decided that this was the Universe's way of giving me the opportunity and nudge to step more fully into being of service in the world. Actually, at the time it felt like a hard shove! Even though I was single and on my own, with no one to support me financially or emotionally, I was willing to take this leap and determined to make it work. Within two weeks, I was officially "self-employed." It was undoubtedly the most scary and stressful time of my life!

With the blessing and help of my former employer, I converted many of the center's clients to my own practice. Although I was grateful for the immediate clients and income from the center, I also had to deal with all the numerous tasks of running a business. I soon realized that being great at my craft was not enough – I had to learn and be great at running a business!

And although I had a marketing degree and nine years' experience working in that field before going to the hypnosis center, what I was learning now about effective marketing for my own business and in today's world was so different. For one thing, the Internet wasn't even available to regular people when I was in college!

Thankfully, I learned enough and worked hard enough to pay my bills and keep my business going doing hypnosis and wellness coaching (weight loss, smoking cessation, fears & phobias, stress, performance improvement, etc.). Working with some amazing business coaches, I figured out a system that really worked for me to increase my earnings every year. But then, that old urge for something more began to surface in the back of my mind.

About five years into my business, I felt a calling to shift the focus and scope of my business to serve more people and on a bigger scale. In talking with my clients and other women I was meeting, I realized that there were many other business owners and entrepreneurs – both new and established – who were spiritually minded, had similar aspirations, experiencing struggles like I once did, and were open to learning and using ALL THREE of the principles that made the difference for me – the Outer Tools (marketing and sales systems), the Inner Tools (mindset), and the Higher Tools (purposeful manifesting). In fact, I was already coaching some of them!

Thus was born the idea for my next metamorphosis – the Marketing, Mindset & Manifesting System. Based on what I had already learned and successfully applied to my business in these three areas – along with the ways I was effectively helping my clients with their businesses – I put together a unique and easy-to-understand system to guide heart-centered, service-based business owners to create a successful business quickly, with less effort and more fun!

So here I am in the next phase of my unconventional life – loving it even more and looking forward to the growth and transitions the Universe still has in store for me. Bring it on!

Lisa Smith, the Marketing, Mindset & Manifesting Coach, helps holistic, service-based business owners get more clients, serve more people, and make more money through practical business tactics and guidance as well as "inner shift" techniques that expose and clear the inner beliefs and gremlins that most don't even realize are playing the major role in keeping them stuck, stressed, and broke.

www.marketingmindsetandmanifesting.com

"What I'd like to impress upon you is that no matter where you come from, where you've been, or what you've been through it doesn't determine where you are heading unless you allow it to."

- Mary Joyce

Making It Possible My Own Way

By Mary Joyce

Looking out my bedroom window while my nine month old crawled around at my feet, it was just a thought in a sea of thoughts that I grabbed hold of for further inspection. That idea became a successful business.

Up until that point my life, I had been living a pretty reactive life with my survival skills having been honed to perfection. I knew enough that my children would never go hungry. At that point in time my life was turning out exactly how I didn't want it to happen, living on a low income while doing everything I could not to lose my mind again.

Once I held onto that thought, an ocean of possibilities opened up. I began to visualise success and what that would look like for me. I realised I already had it all: gorgeous supportive man and two beautiful children, a secure home and tons of previous skills and experiences that would be valuable to others. The only hole in my plan was my zero knowledge of business. I didn't let a small matter of not knowing the "how" stop me, and instead focused on my drive and a passion to make a difference.

What I'd like to impress upon you is that no matter where you come from, where you've been, or what you've been through it doesn't determine where you are heading unless you allow it to.

When I stopped to look at what I had to offer and where the gaps where, I quickly realised that throughout my life I'd always been very resourceful. I began to notice a pattern, one that I'd previously viewed as negative. However, on closer inspection, I began to unravel the uniqueness in my previous strategy. I just figured everyone was like that and knew how to create a vision for their life and make things happen even if they lacked money, time or energy. I soon realised that I created everything in my life: the good, the bad, and the ugly. I had just made unconscious choices and decisions that led me nowhere – only around in circles. I began to tap into my intuition, which was always powerful. However, I didn't fully understand how to harness that power.

So I took an inventory of all my skills, what I was naturally good at, and what I enjoyed doing. I also looked at my previous education and work experience, which had up until that point looked like a random series of bouncing from one diverse job to another with seeming no common thread or strategy. I knew I wanted to work with women. I was already a qualified holistic therapist and had been on a spiritual journey for years so I started looking into coaching. I discovered it was a lot of money to become a qualified coach, money I simply didn't have. Again I was about to let lack of money get in the way.

I knew after I had my second child that going to work for someone else wasn't an option for me. I had my business idea and it took some time for that idea to grow into a profitable business. Before I could launch a coaching business, I had to get the qualifications and knowledge I lacked, so being ever so resourceful and wanting to be home for my babies as much as possible, I set up a massage business. All I needed for that was my hands and some oils, insurance, and some inexpensive start up equipment. With this business I discovered the power of social media as I didn't have a website and ran the whole business off an advert in a free business directory and a Facebook fan page. I very quickly built up a client base of 50 regular customers and began earning a pretty decent income, which I reinvested in my coaching training.

All the while I devoured all of the free business and marketing training available out there. Once I qualified as a coach, I used the same strategy as my previous business and created group programs, which I ran for my local government agencies. I began building a list of subscribers straight away and by this time I had built a website, created freebies, and published a weekly newsletter.

I found that selling massages was a hell of a lot easier than selling coaching as the intangible results were harder to describe when I first started out. I continued educating myself and reading every business book I could get my hands on, sometimes staying up till the early hours of the morning listening to teleseminars, trainings, and anything else I could learn from to make this business a success.

What it lacked was clarity and I just had no sound business. The free stuff I was listening to started to get repetitive and pulling me in all different directions with promises of "Add this vital piece to your business, and you'll be making six figures in no time", and a whole host of other BS statements that people were churning out. I made the decision to join a year-long group program to learn about marketing and business strategy. I couldn't afford it as it cost more than half of my average monthly earnings at that time.

I knew as long as I stayed out of my overdraft every month I would be able to make the payments, as the overdraft would cover the monthly repayments. It was the best investment I ever made. It forced me to truly look at what I was doing and gave me clarity and structure.

I've invested in many programs since then as I've now been running my business for several years and offer my own programs, products, and services. I have a team, and large parts of my business are automated. I work with clients to put structures in place, systemize, and build solid business foundations so they see their vision through to reality.

We all need a helping hand and its less painful and business savvy to do it at the beginning. Why waste a whole lot of time, energy, and money trying to figure it out yourself ending up broke, with your dream becoming a nightmare when you have all the resources at your fingertips?

It was the vision of how I wanted my life to look like that keep me going. I love being able to support my family and creating financial freedom to choose when I work and when I play, all the while changing lives, one person at a time. I wish you every success. Watch your thoughts as they create your reality!

Mary Joyce aka "the Resources Queen" is a gifted intuitive Coach, Speaker, Writer and mum to two beautiful young children. She works with business owners, organizations to maximize their resources, leverage strategic partnerships to grow their tribe and build a solid profitable business.
www.resourcesqueen.com

"I am the architect of my own life and live it on my terms."

- Rachelle Freegard

Be Careful What You Wish For

By Rachelle Freegard

My goal since I was 12 was to be an architect. Not only did I achieve my dream, but I was a partner in a 50-person firm, working on high profile projects nationally. My reality exceeded all my expectations.

Only, I wasn't happy.

In the winter of '07, the overachiever I thought I had perfected in myself was challenged. I was held to a stark light and told my best wasn't good enough. I worked harder and longer every day. Working twelve hours on the weekends and 16 hours on weekdays became the norm. I was at my desk by 8 a.m. at the latest, unless I was at the job site at 7 a.m. I took work home with me after my long day, because I knew there would only be a few hours of sleep before I would awaken in a cold sweat, every molecule trying to explode in my body. I knew if I could just work harder and faster, I would be more than good enough.

After four months of this pattern, I started crying uncontrollably while I was alone, and eventually while I was home, where I didn't need to hold my professional persona. At home, I would continue to work while crying. My business partner went on a one-month vacation, and the associate partner told me to get a handle on my project. For me, this was further recognition of my incompetence to take care of business.

A part of me was dying. I gave up spending time with my family, which means everything to me, because my work integrity was challenged. I stopped using my creative side, to give everything to a war of paper and words. I stopped sleeping to add more work time, which surely did create work that was less than my best. Yet I still needed more work time. Everything would just have to wait.

It was March when I gave my resignation to my partner. My last day would be June 15th. A light at the end of the tunnel kept me going. I knew I would crash when the pace stopped, but I could push myself to do what it took until then. Until about a week before I left, my partners barely acknowledged I was leaving. In fact I was treated as though I would change my mind. I had to hold strong to my conviction that I was leaving.

In April, my body screamed for me to stop. My heart went into tachycardia for most of my day. I was brought to an anxiety level prior to attending a client meeting that almost had me passing out. I begged a partner to attend meetings with me - it rarely happened. I would take someone with me, because I thought I would surely pass out or have a heart attack. In May, I had a heart ablation on a Friday, and returned to work on Monday. The tachycardia was resolved, but the panic and anxiety was not. When I would reach a level of hyperventilation, I would play a game of solitaire on the computer to relax.

Two weeks before my last day, we had a staff meeting. It was easy to say I was leaving for health reasons. They all knew I was in the hospital for a heart procedure. Saying goodbye to the staff was very sad. I had hand-picked most of them. Those I hadn't hired were people I had worked with since I was a staff member. I'm glad many have kept in touch. I'm sorry they didn't get my best performance the last few months we were together.

My schedule lightened the last few days, and I worked only eight hours each day. I started finding time for my needs. I would go out to a nearby deli and pick up lunch (at lunch time!). My first doctor's appointment was a few days before my last day of work. She saw my despair and convinced me to take an anti-depressant, promising me it would be a short-term safety net. She promised me I would be fine. I had to trust her. I wanted to be okay again.

My last day was June 15th. On June 16^{th,} I started reclaiming my place with my family and my home. Leaving my known life for the unknown was frightening, yet it was the best choice. If I had stayed on the same track, I would have no relationships left and my health (or lack thereof) would have continued to decline.

Today I am living on my own schedule. I have many people around me who care. I have my health. My life is full. I am sharing my creative side with the world, living in abundance and loving full on.

I am the architect of my own life and live it on my terms. I am an artist and a writer, and I hold workshops to inspire others to find their true selves. Without reaching bottom, I never would have found myself.

Rachelle Freegard is a sought-after speaker and coach. She has spoken in front of the NAACP, Workers Unions, and Corporations, and now dedicates herself to helping individuals – only 2 or 3 people per calendar quarter. She believes that everyone deserves to live their dreams. With a commitment to your own success, Rachelle will show you how to create an achievable set of goals and use a proven plan to achieve whatever you desire.
www.RachelleFreegard.com

"In order to honor ourselves and our values, we must push ourselves out of our comfort zones and do some scary things. Don't set yourself up for a life of regret. Listen to your heart. Follow your passions."
– Tara DuBois

A Life Unbound From Regret

By Tara DuBois

When you hear your heart calling, answer it. Follow your passions. Live the life you desire without regret or even a second thought to what other people may think.

That's my advice. I try to follow it as often as possible. I have found that more often than not I regret more of the things that I didn't do, or the opportunities that I let pass by, than some of the things that I did do. I love the adventure of putting myself out there and going for it. Out of all of my experiences, I cherish most the times that I held my breath and took the plunge without any idea what would come next.

My life changed when I saw the ocean for the first time. It was love at first sight. Having not ever seen it until adulthood, I instantly wondered how I had ever lived my life without being near it. I was entranced by its sheer enormity and power. I felt an instant connection. I knew then that I had to design a life on the coast.

It must have been serendipity. When my family and I were visiting Oregon as an option for coastal relocation, our real estate agent called. We had a bid on our house. We had to make a decision right there. Do we take the plunge? Do we quit our perfectly good jobs and leave everything we'd built and known to move to a place we'd only experienced for two days?

We did it and took the leap and moved to Oregon. While I won't say the whole process was emotion-free, I can say it all worked out. Sure, there were worries about jobs and schools and housing and all of the other opportunities that come with moving to a completely different environment, but everything just fell beautifully into place. When you get that deep desire for something you have to somehow find a way to make it work. I have absolutely no regrets.

The ocean was less than an hour and a half away from where we lived. My family and I could easily take day trips and did so year-round whenever the mood struck. If I got stressed out, I'd take a visit. Listening to the waves of the ocean would heal my soul and ease my anxieties.

Fast forward a few years and the time came, again, where my soul yearned for something more. I became restless with energy and life was leading me in a different direction that didn't feel quite right. I lived closer to the ocean, but I knew I needed to make major changes in order to find my true bliss. If I didn't make a shift I would regret it.

I asked myself what I really wanted. I knew deep down that I had to strike out on my own professionally and live a life next to the ocean waves. I craved freedom to take charge of "me" and follow my passions and curiosities. Most of all, I wanted to design a lifestyle in which I could live life unbound.

After a few months of planning, I gave notice to my employer, started my own business, and never looked back. I was determined and confident to succeed. Making my dreams a reality depended on it.

I'm still learning every day, but in less than a year, I formed enough client relationships to sustain the business full-time.

I now call the central Oregon coast my home. Instead of having to make a day out of going to the beach, now the sand is just a short walk away. My dream of owning my own business and living footsteps from the water has come true.

My life most definitely changed for the better when I listened to my heart and took action. The ocean was calling me and I am so glad I listened. If I didn't take those leaps I would regret not doing so for the rest of my life.

You see, I don't want to look back late in life and ruminate over missed opportunities and what "might have been." I want to live my life actively on my own volition. I believe that in life you should have freedom to focus on what brings you joy, unbound from obstacles that keep you from realizing your dreams. For me, this means designing a lifestyle that includes blending entrepreneurship with my day-to-day life.

Yes, it's scary. But that's part of growth. In order to honor ourselves and our values, we must push ourselves out of our comfort zones and do some scary things. Don't set yourself up for a life of regret. Listen to your heart. Follow your passions. Live a life unbound!

Tara DuBois dreamed of living a life unbound – free from the structures of the conventional corporate world. Now that she has found independence as an entrepreneur, she wants others to experience joy in what they do as well. Tara helps relieve her clients of the burden of website maintenance and marketing tasks so they can get back to growing your business and doing what they love. Learn more about Tara and her company Unbound Virtual Administrators at www.unboundva.com and find out how she can help you live a life unbound.

Afterword

The authors would like to thank the generous women who shared their wonderful stories with us. Without you and your trust, this book could not be possible.

We would also like to thank Kiva Microfunds for all of the good work that they do in helping deserving women entrepreneurs from all over the globe procure the funds necessary to build their dreams.

We especially thank you, the reader, for picking up this book and letting yourself be inspired by these amazing individuals.

Whether you are about to set off on your own entrepreneurial adventure or just enjoy reading inspiring tales from those who have, we hope that these stories both warmed your heart and challenged your thinking.

Where you go from here is your story. How will you write it?

Don't just dream it. Break free of the traditional mindset. You can live, work, and dream all at once. Whether it's driven by a desire to help others, a specific turning point in your life, a need to fulfill a purpose, or a longing to live a life of your own design – the choice is yours. Don't let your fears hold you back. Embrace your passion and live a life unbound!

About the Editors

Tara DuBois

Tara DuBois dreamed of living a life unbound – free from the structures of the conventional corporate world. Now that she has found independence as an entrepreneur, she wants others to experience joy in what they do as well. Tara helps relieve her clients of the burden of website maintenance tasks so they can get back to growing your business and doing what they love. Learn more about Tara and her company Unbound Virtual Administrators at www.unboundva.com *and find out how she can help you live a life unbound.*

Tara Ursulescu

Tara is a passionate & inspirational writer - with an edge! She is living her dream as the Editor-in-Chief and freelance writer for Soulwoman eMagazine, as one of her many passions includes meeting and interviewing inspirational people and sharing their stories through her writing. Tara has interviewed hundreds of people for various magazines and newspapers, including survivors of natural disasters for a series of television documentaries, "Disasters of the Century", which is still running on The Discovery Channel. Her goal is to inspire others and collect as many perspectives as she can.

John DuBois

John operates Life Unbound Publishing where he helps clients turn their passions into pages. He also creates content for Unbound Virtual Administrators and has articles appearing in The Small Business Owner Magazine and other online publications, John enjoys writing about both business and personal growth. You're likely to find John in front of his laptop with a cup of coffee, but if he's not there he's probably hiking or beachcombing.

Notes

Notes

15076550R00127

Made in the USA
San Bernardino, CA
13 September 2014